Anonymous

History of Maritime Discovery and Adventure

Anonymous

History of Maritime Discovery and Adventure

ISBN/EAN: 9783337177522

Printed in Europe, USA, Canada, Australia, Japan

Cover: Foto ©ninafisch / pixelio.de

More available books at **www.hansebooks.com**

HISTORY

OF

MARITIME DISCOVERY

AND

ADVENTURE.

WILLIAM AND ROBERT CHAMBERS,
LONDON AND EDINBURGH.
1874

NOTICE.

THE present work, reprinted from CHAMBERS'S 'PEOPLE'S EDITIONS,' consists of a collection of some of the most interesting Narratives of Maritime Discovery and Adventure, Tales illustrative of life as it is occasionally and affectingly manifested on the Ocean, and other pieces of a similar character —the whole gathered from the most authentic and respectable sources.

CONTENTS.

	Page
Columbus—Discovery of America,	7
Vasco Nunez de Balboa's Discovery of the Pacific,	20
Adventures of Richard Falconer,	28
The South-sea Marauders,	64
Alexander Selkirk,	73
Perils of a Dutch Crew Wintering at Nova Zembla,	83
Escape from a Shark,	93
Crossing the Line,	95
Adventure with a Whale,	108
Cruise of the Saldanha and Talbot,	113
The Dreadnought,	118
Ross's Expedition,	124
A Cruise in the Baltic,	134
Narrative of the Dee, a Missing Whaler,	142
Adventure in a Voyage to the Levant,	153
An Adventure at Sea,	161
Scene with a Pirate,	166
Mocha Dick, or the White Whale of the Pacific,	176
The Ocean,	191

HISTORY

OF

MARITIME DISCOVERY AND ADVENTURE.

COLUMBUS.—DISCOVERY OF AMERICA.

CHRISTOPHER COLON—better known by his Latinised surname Columbus—was born at Genoa, in 1436. He was the eldest son of a poor wool-carder, and in his early years, may himself, with his brothers, have worked at the trade of his father. His means of education were of course limited; but it is known that, at an early age, he had made some progress in the study of mathematics and the Latin language. While a youth, he was very fond of reading all works upon geography, and directed his attention entirely to those branches of learning which would be of use to him in the pursuits to which he had already determined to devote his life. He spent a short time at the college of Padua, where he acquired a knowledge of astronomy and other sciences most necessary to seamen, and particularly useful at a time when so little progress had been made in the art of navigation.

Columbus left the university of Padua when he was about fourteen years of age. Of the events which immediately followed, we have no accurate information. It is only known that he began life in the humble capacity of a sailor boy, on board one of the Genoese vessels which sailed in the Mediterranean, and from which station he rose by his ability to be commander of a vessel. Subsequently, about the year 1470, he visited

Lisbon, and there married a young lady of the name of Palestrello, the daughter of an Italian who had been on several voyages of discovery under Prince Henry of Portugal. From her Columbus obtained the journals and charts which had been drawn up by her father on his various voyages. He made inquiries about the voyages of the Portuguese along the coast of Guinea, in Africa, and delighted to converse with the sailors who had been there. At this period there was no knowledge of any land farther westward than Madeira, the Canaries, and Cape Verde, with the islands of that name, all lying off the west coast of Africa, and in the track of vessels sailing from Europe to India by the Cape of Good Hope. The Atlantic, within the eastern verge of which these islands lie, was supposed by mariners to be a boundless ocean to the west, or that it was limited only by Japan, India, and other portions of the Asiatic continent. By pondering on the figure of the globe, and reasoning from conjecture, Columbus became convinced, that if vessels were to sail westward on the Atlantic, islands would certainly be found in that direction, or that India might be reached much more easily by that route than by sailing thither eastward by the Cape of Good Hope. While his mind was occupied by these reflections, he became naturalised in Portugal, and made several voyages to Guinea and the Canaries, by which he improved himself in navigation. When residing at home, as we are told, he supported his family, including his father and younger brothers, by drawing maps and charts. He also lived very temperately, was plain in his dress, and rigorously observant of his religious duties.

As soon as Columbus had completely formed his opinions regarding the discovery of land in the Atlantic, he considered it necessary to put himself under the patronage of some European power, which should furnish him with a vessel or vessels, and all other requisite means for making good the discovery. It would be very painful to recite minutely the steps he took on this occasion. He applied first to the Portuguese monarch,

John II., by whom he was used exceedingly ill. Mortified by the treatment he had received, he in the year 1484 privately departed from Portugal with his son Diego; his wife having been some time dead. Before leaving Portugal, he sent his brother Bartholomew to make proposals to the King of England, Henry VII., but Bartholomew was unfortunately captured by pirates on the way to England, which he did not reach till the propositions of Columbus had been accepted by another power.

On leaving Portugal, Columbus betook himself to Spain, with the intention of laying his plans before Ferdinand and Isabella, who at that time governed the united Spanish kingdoms of Castile and Arragon. Columbus arrived at Palos, a small sea-port in Spain, towards the end of the year 1485, and, as it would appear, in a somewhat destitute condition. About half a league from Palos there was a convent of Franciscan friars. Columbus, with his little son, stopped one day at this convent, to ask for some bread and water. The prior of the monastery, Juan Perez de Marchena, was a man of intelligence and learning. Being struck with the appearance and demeanour of Columbus, he immediately entered into conversation with him. It ended in an invitation to the stranger to become for a while a guest at the convent. Juan Perez talked with Columbus of his plans, and became exceedingly interested in them. He sent for a scientific friend, Garcia Fernandez, the physician of Palos, with whom the matter was industriously examined. All became more and more zealous in their wishes and hopes for putting the project into execution. It happened that Juan Perez was an intimate friend of Fernando de Talavera, the confessor of Queen Isabella. Columbus being furnished with a letter of introduction to Talavera, in which his enterprise was strenuously recommended to the patronage of the crown, he left his son at the convent with his friend, and departed for the court of Castile, in the spring of 1486.

On arriving at Cordova, where the court at that time

was residing, he found it almost impossible to obtain a hearing. This he at length accomplished; but it was long before he could make a sufficient impression on Ferdinand or his queen to induce them to second his views. They referred his suit to a body of learned professors, who laughed at his project, which they declared to be irreligious and impious.

Tired with waiting on the pleasure of the court of Spain, and receiving a letter of encouragement from the court of France, Columbus departed on a journey to Paris, taking in his way the friendly convent at Palos, where he had left his son under the care of Juan Perez. When his old friend the prior saw Columbus once more at the gate of his monastery, after several years of vain solicitation at court, he was deeply affected. He entreated him by all means to remain in the country. He had been father confessor to the queen, and thought he might still exercise an influence over her mind. He accordingly proceeded to Santa Fé, where the sovereigns were in person superintending the siege of the capital of Granada. Perez obtained a ready access to the queen. He laid before her the propositions of Columbus with freedom and eloquence. Isabella was moved with the grandeur of the project. The principles upon which it was founded, the advantages that would result from its success, and the glory it would shed upon Spain, were for the first time represented to her in their true colours. She promised her patronage to the undertaking.

It was now only necessary to agree upon the terms. Columbus would listen only to princely conditions. A meaner spirit, after years of unsuccessful toil, poverty, and disappointment, would have been glad to secure the assistance of the sovereigns, on such arrangements as their own liberality might dictate. But Columbus proposed his own rewards and honours, and would consent to no other. He demanded them as if he were already successful, and aware of the extent and importance of his discoveries. The court were eventually obliged to grant that he should be admiral on the ocean, and enjoy all the privileges and honours allowed to the high admiral of Castile; that he should be governor over all the countries he might discover; and that he should reserve to himself one-tenth of all pearls, precious stones, gold, silver, and articles of merchandise, in whatever manner obtained, within his admiralty. They also allowed that he should appoint judges in all parts of Spain trading to those countries; and that on this voyage, and at all other times, he should contribute an eighth part of the expense, and receive an eighth part of the profits. These articles of agreement were signed by Ferdinand and Isabella, at the city of Santa Fé, on the 17th of August 1492. Three caravels, or very small vessels, little better than decked boats, were procured at Palos, and orders given that they should be manned and provided with all care and diligence. There were still difficulties before commencing the voyage, which it required all the perseverance of Columbus to overcome. It was almost impossible to prevail upon any seamen to engage in the undertaking. The royal order for the fitting out of the caravels was peremptory; but weeks passed, and it still remained unfulfilled. The old sailors who had passed most of their lives upon the water, shrank from the enterprise with horror. New orders were issued by the court, and officers were appointed to press ships and seamen into the service of Columbus. This measure occasioned a great deal of disputing and confusion, but led to no important result. At length, a rich and adventurous navigator, named Alonzo Pinzon, came forward, and interested himself very strenuously in the expedition. His assistance was effectual. He owned vessels, and had many seamen in his employ, and consequently possessed great influence. He and his brother Vicente Pinzon determined to take commands, and sail with Columbus. Their example had a great effect; they persuaded their relations and friends to embark with them, and the vessels were ready for sea within a month after they had thus engaged in their equipment.

We now find Columbus on the eve of his first grand expedition, which was to result in the discovery of the

American continent and islands. The simple seaman of Genoa, whom the ignorant derided as a fool, and philosophers neglected as an impostor, after years of poverty and disappointment, had at length obtained the object of his unwearied solicitations, and was going forward with a calm and dignified assurance of success. What unspeakable joy must have filled his heart, as the little caravel in which he sailed was leaving the shores of Spain in the distance, stretching forward into that dim and unexplored ocean, from whose shadows he was to reveal new dominions for his country, and a new world for Europe!

Columbus and his companions sailed from the bar of Saltes, a small island in front of the town of Huelva, early on the morning of the 3d of August 1492. They directed their course in a south-westerly direction for the Canary Islands. These they reached; and after spending some time in repairing a damage in one of the vessels, and taking in fresh supplies of wood, water, and meat, set sail from the harbour of Gomera on the 6th of September. They steered their course directly west. In a few days they began to fall in with what Columbus considered signs of land, such as quantities of green weeds, a live crab, flocks of birds, and so forth; but all these signs of land continually failed. The crews, daily more and more disposed to murmur against the admiral, had by turns to be flattered and threatened with punishment, to keep them from open rebellion. Provisions at length were falling short, and some of the men proposed to throw Columbus into the sea, and give out on their return that he had accidentally fallen overboard.

The first land that Columbus expected to meet was Cipango, which had been placed by geographers at the eastern extremity of India. This was the name given to the island now called Japan, by Marco Polo, a Venetian traveller. The most extravagant accounts of the riches of this country were given by the writers of that age, and the admiral was anxious to proceed directly thither. At sunrise, on Sunday the 7th of October, the Nina, which had outsailed the other vessels, on account of her swiftness, hoisted a flag at her mast-head, and fired a gun, as a signal of having discovered land. There had been a reward promised by the king and queen to the man who should first make this discovery, and each of the vessels was striving very eagerly to get ahead, and obtain the promised recompence. As they found nothing of the land the Nina had made signals for, the admiral shifted his course, about evening, towards the west-south-west, with a determination to sail two days in that direction. The reason for making this change was an observation which had been made in watching the flight of birds. The Portuguese had discovered most of their islands in this manner, and Columbus noticed that the flocks which passed them all flew from the north to the south-west. He inferred from this that land was situated in that quarter. After sailing a day or two, they found the air as soft as that of Seville in April, and so fragrant that it was delicious to breathe it. The weeds appeared very fresh, and many land birds were taken. The men, however, had lost all faith in any signs of land. They did not cease to murmur and complain. The admiral encouraged them in the best manner he could, representing the riches they were about to acquire, and adding, that it was to no purpose to complain; for, having come so far, they had nothing to do but to continue, till, by the assistance of Heaven, they should arrive at the Indies.

On the 11th of October, they met with signs of land that could not be mistaken, and all began to regain spirits and confidence. The crew of the Pinta saw a cane and a log. They also picked up a stick, which appeared to have been carved with an iron instrument, a small board, and abundance of weeds that had been newly washed from the banks. The crew of the Nina saw other similar signs, and found, besides, a branch of a thorn full of red berries. Convinced by these tokens of the neighbourhood of land, Columbus, after evening prayers, made an address to his crew, reminding them of the mercy of God in bringing them so long a voyage with such fair weather, and encouraging them by signs that were every day plainer and plainer. He repeated the instructions he had given at the Canary Islands, that when they had sailed seven hundred leagues to the westward without discovering land, they should lie by from midnight till daybreak. He told them that, as they had strong hopes of finding land that night, every one should watch in his place; and besides the thirty crowns a-year which the Spanish sovereigns had promised to the first discoverer, he would give him a velvet doublet.

About ten o'clock that evening, while Columbus was keeping an anxious look-out from the top of the cabin, he thought he beheld a light glimmering at a great distance. Fearing that his hopes might deceive him, he called two of his companions to confirm him. One of them came in time to observe it, but the other was too late. It had disappeared. From this they supposed it might be the torch of some fisherman, raised up and then suddenly dropped again. They were all confident of being near land. About two o'clock in the morning the Pinta gave the signal of land, which was first perceived by a sailor named Rodrigo de Triana.

When the day appeared, they perceived before them a large island, quite level, full of green trees and delicious waters, and to all appearance thickly inhabited. Numbers of the people immediately collected, and ran down to the shore. They were very much astonished at the sight of the ships, which they believed to be living creatures. The ships immediately came to anchor. The admiral went ashore in his boat, well armed, and bearing the royal standard. The other captains each took a banner of the Green Cross, containing the initials of the names of the king and queen on each side, and a crown over each letter. The admiral called upon the two captains, and the rest of the crew who landed, to bear witness that he took possession of that island for his sovereigns. They all gave thanks to God, kneeling upon the shore, shedding tears of joy for the great mercy received. The admiral rose, and called the island San Salvador. The Indians called it Guanahani, and it is now called Cat Island. It belongs to that group called the Bahamas.

Many of the natives came down to witness this ceremony. They were very peaceable and quiet people, and the admiral gave them some red caps, glass beads, and a few other trifles of small value, with which they were very much delighted. They imagined that the strangers had descended from heaven, and valued the slightest token they could receive from them as of immense worth. When the admiral and his companions returned to their vessels, the natives followed them in large numbers. Some swam; others went in their canoes, carrying parrots, spun cotton, javelins, and other articles, to exchange for hawks' bells and strings of beads. They went entirely naked, seeming to be very poor and simple.

In the morning, Columbus sailed along the coast of the island towards the north-west, and in his voyage discovered other islands, to which he gave names. The largest he fell in with was Cuba, which is nearly as large as Great Britain. At Cuba he expected to find a great trade, abundance of gold and spices, large ships, and rich merchants. He inferred that this must be the island of Cipango, of which Marco Polo had said so many marvellous things. In these conjectures he was entirely mistaken. On the 5th of December, he discovered and landed upon another large island, which he called Hispaniola, now named St Domingo or Hayti. Here he planted a fort, which he made the seat of a colony. From this period may be dated the commencement of the misfortunes of Columbus. That great man now lost control over his wicked and rapacious companions, who seemed desirous of plundering the newly discovered islands, and afterwards of sailing home, to be the first to make known the discoveries that had been made. Pinzon, the commander of the Pinta, took the lead in these dastardly proceedings, for which he afterwards expressed the deepest regret.

After cruising about for some time, and endeavouring to enter into friendly alliances with native chiefs in the islands, Columbus set sail with his vessels on his return to Spain. His homeward voyage was exceedingly stormy; and after braving the most imminent dangers, came in sight of land near Lisbon, on the 4th of March 1493. Having paid his respects, in passing, to the Portuguese monarch, he proceeded without loss of time towards the coast of Spain; and on the 15th of March, he entered and anchored in the harbour of Palos. The joy and confusion excited in Palos by the arrival of Columbus may be easily imagined. He was every where received with shouts and acclamations, and such honours as were usually paid to sovereigns.

After the first expressions of joy and admiration, Columbus departed for Seville. From this place he sent a message to Barcelona, where the king and queen at that time resided, to lay before them a brief account of his voyage, and to receive from them an indication of their royal will. His reception at Barcelona was particularly gratifying. He made a sort of triumphal entry, surrounded by knights and nobles, who emulated each other in their efforts to swell his praises. He was received publicly by the sovereigns, in a splendid saloon, seated on the throne, and encircled by a magnificent court. On his entrance, they rose to greet him, and would hardly allow him to kiss their hands, considering it too unworthy a mark of vassalage. Columbus then gave an account of his discoveries, and exhibited the different articles which he had brought home with him. He described the quantity of spices, the promise of gold, the fertility of the soil, the delicious climate, the never-fading verdure of the trees, the brilliant plumage of the birds, in the new regions which his own enterprise had acquired for his sovereigns. He then drew their attention to six natives of the New World, whom he had brought, and who were present, and described their manners and dispositions. He exhibited their dresses and ornaments, their rude utensils, their feeble arms, which corresponded with his description of them, as naked and ignorant barbarians. To this he added, that he had observed no traces of idolatry or superstition among them, and that they all seemed to be convinced of the existence of a Supreme Being. The conclusion of his speech was in these words: "That God had reserved for the Spanish monarchs, not only all the treasures of the New World, but a still greater treasure, of inestimable value, in the infinite number of souls destined to be brought over into the bosom of the Christian church."

After he had finished his address, the whole assembly fell upon their knees, while an anthem was chanted by the choir of the royal chapel. With songs of praise, the glory was given to God for the discovery of a New World. Columbus and his adventures were for many days the wonder and delight of the people and the court. The sovereigns admitted the admiral to their audience at all hours, and loaded him with every mark of favour and distinction. Men of the highest rank were proud of the honour of his company.

All matters were soon prepared for the second expedition to the New World. On the dawn of the 25th of September 1493, the Bay of Cadiz was crowded with the departing fleet of Columbus. There were three large ships and fourteen caravels waiting for the signal to sail. All on board were breathing hope and joy. Instead of the gloomy despondency that overshadowed the leave-taking at Palos, there was now animation and cheerfulness. The whole fleet was under way before the rising of the sun, sailing joyfully, under a serene sky, through the tranquil waters.

During this second voyage, Columbus extended his discoveries, though without reaping any solid advantage to himself. He found the fort which he had planted entirely destroyed, and the men whom he had left slain, their avaricious and quarrelsome disposition having led to their extirpation by the enraged natives. A new colony under better auspices was, however, settled, and the payment of a tribute by the natives enforced. In the mean time, the disaffected and worthless among his companions carried groundless complaints against Columbus to the court of Spain, and he returned to obtain reparation of the injurious imputations. On appearing before his sovereigns, he was soothed by some trifling apologies, and dispatched on a third voyage in May 1498, and in this expedition he landed on the coast of Paria, in South America. He found the lately discovered islands distracted with the horrors of civil discord. The vices of the settlers he had left had produced misery and despair, and the unfortunate Columbus was loudly accused of being the cause of the universal ruin. His enemies in Spain had likewise the influence to induce the dispatch of a commissioner, one Bovadilla, to Hispaniola, to inquire into the truth of the charges against Columbus, and to supersede his administration. The consequence of this harsh procedure was, that Columbus, with his brothers Diego and Bartholomew, after being treated with the utmost indignity, were sent to Spain in chains.

The rumour was no sooner circulated at Cadiz and Seville that Columbus and his brothers had arrived, loaded with chains, and condemned to death, than it gave rise to a burst of public indignation. The excitement was strong and universal, and messengers were immediately dispatched to convey the intelligence to Ferdinand and Isabella. The sovereigns were moved by this exhibition of popular feeling, and were offended that their name and authority should have been used to sanction such dishonourable violence. They gave orders for the immediate liberation of the prisoners, and for their being escorted to Granada with the respect and honour they deserved. They annulled all the processes against them without examination, and promised an ample punishment for all their wrongs. Columbus was not, however, restored to his command at Hispaniola, nor was it till many months afterwards that he was placed at the head of an expedition to open a new passage to the East Indies. On the 9th of May 1502, Columbus again set sail from Cadiz on a fourth voyage of discovery. During this voyage he touched at some parts of the South American continent, and also at some of the formerly discovered islands; but he failed in making any important discoveries, in consequence of the bad state of his vessels, which were old and unfit for sailing. With a squadron reduced to a single vessel, he now returned to Spain, where he heard with regret of the death of his patron Isabella. This was a sad blow to his expectations of redress and remuneration. Ferdinand was jealous and ungrateful. He was weary of a man who had conferred so much glory on his kingdom, and unwilling to repay him with the honours and privileges his extraordinary services so richly merited. Columbus, therefore, sank into obscurity, and was reduced to such straitened circumstances, that, according to his own account, he had no place to repair to except an inn, and very frequently had not wherewithal to pay his reckoning. Disgusted and mortified by the base conduct of Ferdinand, and exhausted with the hardships which he had suffered, and oppressed with infirmities, Columbus ended his life at Valladolid, on the 20th of May 1506. He died with a composure of mind suitable to the magnanimity which distinguished his character, and with sentiments of piety becoming that supreme respect for religion, which he manifested in every occurrence of his life.

The monument erected by Ferdinand to his memory bears this inscription:—

"Por Castilla y por Leon
Nuevo Mundo hallo Colon."

Which may be thus translated:—

"For Castile and Leon Columbus found a New World."

The discoveries of Columbus laid open a knowledge of what are now termed the West India Islands, and a small portion of the South American continent, which this great navigator, till the day of his death, believed to be a part of Asia or India. About ten years after his decease, the real character of America and its islands became known to European navigators; and by a casual circumstance, one of these adventurers, *Amerigo* Vespucii, a Florentine, had the honour of conferring the name *America* upon a division of the globe, which in justice ought to have been called after the unfortunate Columbus.

VASCO NUNEZ DE BALBOA'S DISCOVERY OF THE PACIFIC.

THE latter days of Columbus, as will have been observed from his melancholy history, were embittered by the turbulence of his fellow-adventurers, who succeeded him in his command, and deprived him of the lustre belonging to his valuable services. Among those ambitious and discontented but brave Spaniards, few were an equal match to Vasco Nunez de Balboa, either for the command which he obtained over his associates or for his daring intrepidity in facing danger. We learn from an exceedingly agreeable volume, entitled, " The Voyages of the Companions of Columbus," * that this man was one of the most enterprising of those commanders, appointed by Spain in taking charge of the colony at Darien. He was never tired of levying war against the caciques, or petty native princes, and it was on one of his expeditions of this nature, when extorting gold from one of the simple inhabitants, that he received intelligence of the existence of the great Pacific Ocean at no very great distance on the opposite side of the country. In the government of the colony, Vasco Nunez does not appear to have been much-actuated by principles of moderation or justice. By his audacious conduct he at length roused the indignation of the Spanish sovereign, and was condemned in certain damages. Informed of this storm, which had arisen in consequence of the complaints laid against him, and that he would be immediately summoned to the court of Spain, to answer the criminal charge advanced against him, he at once resolved on the means to be adopted for his protection.

Vasco Nunez (says the author) was at first stunned by this intelligence, which seemed at one blow to anni-

* Family Library, 1832.

hilate all his hopes and fortunes. He was a man, however, of prompt decision and intrepid spirit. The information received from Spain was private and informal; no order had yet arrived from the king; he was still master of his actions, and had control over the colony. One brilliant achievement might atone for all the past, and fix him in the favour of the monarch. Such an achievement was within his reach—the discovery of the southern sea. It is true, a thousand soldiers had been required for the expedition; but were he to wait for their arrival from Spain, his day of grace would be past. It was a desperate thing to undertake the task with the handful of men at his command, but the circumstances of the case were desperate. Fame, fortune, life itself, depended upon the successful and the prompt execution of the enterprise. To linger was to be lost.

Vasco Nunez looked round upon the crew of daring and reckless adventurers that formed the colony, and chose one hundred and ninety of the most resolute, vigorous, and devoted to his person. These he armed with swords, targets, cross-bows, and arquebuses. He did not conceal from them the danger of the enterprise into which he was about to lead them: but the spirit of these Spanish adventurers was always roused by the idea of perilous and extravagant exploit. To aid his slender forces, he took with him a number of bloodhounds, which had been found to be terrific allies in Indian warfare.

The Spanish writers make particular mention of one of those animals, named Leoncico, which was a constant companion, and, as it were, body-guard of Vasco Nunez, and describe him as minutely as they would a favourite warrior. He was of a middle size, but immensely strong: of a dull-yellow or reddish colour, with a black muzzle, and his body was scarred all over with wounds received in innumerable battles with the Indians. Vasco Nunez always took him on his expeditions, and sometimes lent him to others, receiving for his services the same share of booty allotted to an armed man. In this way he gained by him in the course of his campaigns upwards of a thousand crowns. The Indians, it is said, had conceived such terror of this animal, that the very sight of him was sufficient to put a host of them to flight.

In addition to these forces, Vasco Nunez took with him a number of the Indians of Darien, whom he had won to him by kindness, and whose services were important, from their knowledge of the wilderness, and of the habits and resources of savage life. Such was the motley armament that set forth from the little colony of Darien, under the guidance of a daring, if not desperate commander, in quest of the great Pacific Ocean.

It was on the 1st of September that Vasco Nunez embarked with his followers in a brigantine and nine large canoes or pirogues, followed by the cheers and good wishes of those who remained at the settlement. Standing to the north-westward, he arrived without accident at Coyba, the dominion of the cacique Careta, whose daughter he had received as a pledge of amity. That Indian beauty had acquired a great influence over Vasco Nunez, and appears to have cemented his friendship with her father and her people. He was received by the cacique with open arms, and furnished with guides and warriors to aid him in his enterprises.

Vasco Nunez left about half of his men at Coyba to guard the brigantine and canoes, while he should penetrate the wilderness with the residue. The importance of his present expedition, not merely as affecting his own fortunes, but as it were unfolding a mighty secret of nature, seems to have impressed itself upon his spirit, and to have given correspondent solemnity to his conduct. Before setting out upon his march, he caused mass to be performed, and offered up prayers to God for the success of his perilous undertaking.

It was on the 6th of September that he struck off for the mountains. The march was difficult and toilsome in the extreme. The Spaniards, encumbered with the weight of their armour and weapons, and oppressed by the heat of a tropical climate, were obliged to climb rocky precipices, and to struggle through close and tangled forests. Their Indian allies aided them by carrying their ammunition and provisions, and by guiding them to the most practicable paths.

On the 8th of September they arrived at the village of Ponca, the ancient enemy of Careta. The village was lifeless and abandoned; the cacique and his people had fled to the fastnesses of the mountains. The Spaniards remained here several days to recruit the health of some of their number who had fallen ill. It was necessary also to procure guides acquainted with the mountain wilderness they were approaching. The retreat of Ponca was at length discovered, and he was prevailed upon, though reluctantly, to come to Vasco Nunez. The latter had a peculiar facility in winning the confidence and friendship of the natives. The cacique was soon so captivated by his kindness, that he revealed to him in secret all he knew of the natural riches of the country. He assured him of the truth of what had been told him about a great pechry or sea beyond the mountains, and gave him several ornaments ingeniously wrought of fine gold, which had been brought from the countries upon its borders. He told him, moreover, that when he had attained the summit of a lofty ridge, to which he pointed, and which seemed to rise up to the skies, he would behold that sea spread out far below him.

Animated by the accounts, Vasco Nunez procured fresh guides from the cacique, and prepared to ascend the mountains. Numbers of his men having fallen ill from fatigue and the heat of the climate, he ordered them to return slowly to Coyba, taking with him none but such as were in robust and vigorous health. On the 20th of September, he again set forward through a broken rocky country, covered with a matted forest, and intersected by deep and turbulent streams, many of which it was necessary to cross upon rafts. So toilsome was the journey, that in four days they did not advance above ten leagues, and in the meantime they suffered excessively from hunger. At the end of this time they arrived at the province of a warlike cacique, named Quaraqua, who was at war with Ponca.

Hearing that a band of strangers were entering his territories, guided by subjects of his inveterate foe, the cacique took the field with a great number of warriors, some armed with bows and arrows, others with long spears, or with double-handed maces of palm-wood, almost as heavy and hard as iron. Seeing the inconsiderable number of the Spaniards, they set upon them with furious yells, thinking to overcome them in an instant. The first discharge of fire-arms, however, struck them with dismay. They thought they were contending with demons who vomited forth thunder and lightning, especially when they saw their companions fall bleeding and dead beside them, without receiving any apparent blow. They took to headlong flight, and were hotly pursued by the Spaniards and their bloodhounds. Some were transfixed with lances, others hewn down with swords, and many were torn to pieces by the dogs, so that Quaraqua and 600 of his warriors were left dead upon the field. After this sanguinary triumph, the Spaniards marched to the village of Quaraqua, where they found considerable booty in gold and jewels. Of this Vasco Nunez reserved one-fifth for the crown, and shared the rest liberally among his followers. The village was at the foot of the last mountain that remained for them to climb; several of the Spaniards, however, were so disabled by the wounds they had received in battle, or so exhausted by the fatigue and hunger they had endured, that they were unable to proceed. They were obliged, therefore, reluctantly to remain in the village, within sight of the mountain-top that commanded the long-sought prospect. Vasco Nunez selected fresh guides from among his prisoners who were natives of the province, and sent back the subjects of Ponca. Of the band of Spaniards who had set out with him in this enterprise, 67 alone remained in sufficient health and spirits for this last effort. These he ordered to retire early to repose, that they might be ready to set off at the cool and fresh hour of daybreak, so as to reach the summit of the mountain before the noon-tide heat.

The day had scarce dawned, when Vasco Nunez and his followers set forth from the Indian village, and began to climb the height. It was a severe and rugged toil for men so wayworn; but they were filled with new ardour at the idea of the triumphant scene that was so soon to repay them for all their hardships. About ten o'clock in the morning they emerged from the thick forests through which they had hitherto struggled, and arrived at a lofty and airy region of the mountain. The bald summit alone remained to be ascended; and their guides pointed to a moderate eminence, from which they said the southern sea was visible.

Upon this, Vasco Nunez commanded his followers to halt, and that no man should stir from this place. Then, with a palpitating heart, he ascended alone the bare mountain-top. On reaching the summit, the long-desired prospect burst upon his view. It was as if a new world were unfolded to him, separated from all hitherto known by this mighty barrier of mountains. Below him extended a vast chaos of rock and forest, and green savannahs and wandering streams, while at a distance the waters of the promised ocean glittered in the morning sun.

At this glorious prospect, Vasco Nunez sank upon his knees, and poured out thanks to God for being the first European to whom it was given to make that great discovery. He then called his people to ascend: " Behold, my friends," said he, " that glorious sight which we have so much desired. Let us give thanks to God that he has granted us this great honour and advantage. Let us pray to him to guide and aid us to conquer the sea and land which we have discovered, and which Christian has never entered to preach the holy doctrine of the Evangelists. As to yourselves, be as you have hitherto been, faithful and true to me, and by the favour of Christ you will become the richest Spaniards that have ever come to the Indies; you will render the greatest services to your king that ever vassal rendered to his lord; and you will have the eternal glory and advantage of all that is discovered, conquered, and converted to our holy Catholic faith."

The Spaniards answered this speech by embracing Vasco Nunez, and promising to follow him to death. Among them was a priest, named Andres de Vara, who lifted up his voice and chanted *Te Deum laudamus*—the usual anthem of Spanish discoverers. The rest, kneeling down, joined in the strain with pious enthusiasm and tears of joy; and never did a more sincere oblation rise to the Deity from a sanctified altar than from that wild mountain summit. It was indeed one of the most sublime discoveries that had yet been made in the New World, and must have opened a boundless field of conjecture to the wondering Spaniards. The imagination delights to picture forth the splendid confusion of their thoughts. Was this the great Indian Ocean, studded with precious islands, abounding in gold, in gems, and spices, and bordered by the gorgeous cities and wealthy marts of the east? or was it some lonely sea locked up in the embraces of savage uncultivated continents, and never traversed by a bark, excepting the light pirogue of the savage? The latter could hardly be the case, for the natives had told the Spaniards of golden realms, and populous and powerful and luxurious nations upon its shores. Perhaps it might be bordered by various people, civilised in fact, though differing from Europe in their civilisation—who might have peculiar laws and customs, and arts and sciences—who might form, as it were, a world of their own, intercommuning by this mighty sea, and carrying on commerce between their own islands and continents, but who might exist in total ignorance and independence of the other hemisphere.

Such may naturally have been the ideas suggested by the sight of this unknown ocean. It was the prevalent belief of the Spaniards, however, that they were the first Christians who had made the discovery. Vasco Nunez, therefore, called upon all present to witness that he took possession of that sea, its islands, and surrounding lands, in the name of the sovereigns of Castile ; and the notary of the expedition made a testimonial of the same, to which all present, to the number of sixty-seven men, signed their names. He then caused a fair and tall tree to be cut down, and wrought into a cross, which was elevated on the spot from whence he had first beheld the sea. A mound of stones was likewise piled up to serve as a monument, and the names of the Castilian sovereigns were carved on the neighbouring trees. The Indians beheld all these ceremonials and rejoicings in silent wonder, and, while they aided to erect the cross and pile up the mound of stones, marvelled exceedingly at the meaning of these monuments, little thinking that they marked the subjugation of their land.

The memorable event here recorded took place on the 26th of September 1513, so that the Spaniards had spent twenty days in performing the journey from the province of Creta to the summit of the mountain, a distance which at present, it is said, does not require more than six days' travel. Indeed, the isthmus in this neighbourhood is not more than eighteen leagues in breadth, in its widest part, and in some places only seven ; but it consists of a ridge of extremely high and rugged mountains. When the discoverers traversed it, they had no route but the Indian paths, and often had to force their way amidst all kinds of obstacles, both from the savage country and its savage inhabitants. In fact, the details of this narrative sufficiently account for the slowness of their progress, and present an array of difficulties and perils, which, as has been well observed, none but those "men of iron" could have subdued and overcome.

ADVENTURES OF RICHARD FALCONER.*
PART I.

I was born at Bruton, a market-town in Somersetshire, of parents tolerably well to pass in the world. My mother died when I was very young: my father had been a great traveller in his youth, and frequently repeating his adventures abroad, I had a great desire to follow his steps. I often begged he would let me go to sea with some captain of his acquaintance; but he would reply, " Stay where you are; you know not the hazards and dangers that attend a sea life ; think no more of going to sea, for I know it is only the desire of youth, prone to change ; and if I should give you leave, one week's voyage would make you wish to be at home again." I used all the arguments I could think of to move my father from this opposition, but without effect. [At length, in consequence of certain family misfortunes, the father gave his consent to the departure of Richard, who proceeded to Bristol, and by the recommendation of his parent to a Captain Pultney, was put on board the Albion frigate, Captain Wase commander ; it was a trader bound to Jamaica, and set sail with a fair wind on the 2d of May 1699. The vessel reached its destination in safety after a stormy voyage ; what occurred next is narrated as follows :—]

Now, finding our affairs would detain us half a year

* These Adventures are reprinted, with some very slight alterations, from a rare old work, now little known, but which has latterly been republished by a London bookseller. It is worth while to note that the work was a favourite with Sir Walter Scott, in his younger days, as appears from the following observations made by him on the fly-leaf of a copy which had been in his possession :—" This book I read in early youth. I am ignorant whether it is altogether fictitious and written upon De Foe's plan, which it generally resembles, or whether it is only an exaggerated account of the adventures of a real person. It is very scarce; for endeavouring to add it to the other favourites of my infancy, I think I looked for it ten years to no purpose, and at last owed it to the active kindness of Mr Terry; yet Richard Falconer's adventures seem to have passed through several editions."

longer, I obtained leave of the captain to go in a sloop, with some of my acquaintances, to get logwood on the South American coast, at the Bay of Campeachy; and on the 25th of September we set sail on this expedition. The manner of getting this wood is as follows:—A company of desperate fellows go together in a sloop, well armed, and land by stealth [to avoid an encounter with the Spaniards, to whom the country at that time belonged]; but in case of any resistance, the whole crew attend on the cutters ready armed, to defend them. We sailed merrily on our course for six days together, with a fair wind towards the bay; but on the seventh, the clouds darkened, and the welkin seemed all on fire with lightning, and the thunder roared louder than ever I heard it in my life. In short, a dreadful hurricane approached. The sailors had furled their sails and lowered their topmasts, waiting for it under a double-reefed foresail. At length it came with extreme violence, which lasted three hours, until it insensibly abated, and brought on a stark calm. We then loosed our sails in expectation of the wind, which stole out again in about half an hour. About six in the evening we saw a waterspout, an aërial cloud that draws up the salt water of the sea, and distils it into fresh showers of rain. This cloud comes down in the form of a pipe of lead, of a vast thickness, and, by the force of the sun, sucks up a great quantity of water. I stood an hour to observe it. After it had continued about half an hour in the water, it drew up insensibly, by degrees, till it was lost in the clouds; but in closing, it shut out some of the water, which fell into the sea again, with a noise like that of thunder, and occasioned a smoke in the water that continued for a considerable time.

October the 6th, we anchored at Trist island, in the Bay of Campeachy, and sent our men ashore at Logwood Creek, to seek for the logwood cutters, who immediately came on board. The bargain was soon struck; and in exchange for our rum and sugar, and a little money, we got in our lading in eight days, and set sail for Jamaica on the 15th day of October. Now, getting up to Jamaica, again, generally takes up two months, because we are obliged to ply it all the way to windward. I one day went down into the hold to bottle off a small parcel of wine I had there; coming upon deck again, I wanted to wash myself, but did not care to go into the water, so went into the boat astern that we had hoisted out in the morning to look after a wreck. Having washed and dressed myself, I took a book out of my pocket, and sat reading in the boat; when, before I was aware, a storm began to rise, so that I could not get up the ship's side as usual, but called for the ladder of ropes that hangs over the ship's quarter, in order to get up that way; whether it broke through rottenness, as being seldom used, I cannot tell, but down I fell into the sea: and though the ship tacked about to take me up, yet I lost sight of them, through the duskiness of the evening, and the storm. I had the most dismal fears that could ever possess any one in my condition. I was forced to drive with the wind, which, by good fortune, set in with the current; and having kept myself above water, as near as I could guess in this fright, four hours, I felt my feet every now and then touch the ground; and at last, by a great wave, I was thrown and left upon the sand; yet, it being dark, I knew not what to do; but I got up and walked as well as my tired limbs would let me, and every now and then was overtaken by the waves, which were not high enough to wash me away. When I had got far enough, as I thought, to be out of danger, I could not discover any thing of land, and I immediately conjectured that it was but some bank of sand, that the sea would overflow at high tide. Whereupon I sat down to rest my weary limbs, and fit myself for death; for that was all I could expect, in my own opinion: then all my sins came flying in my face. I offered up fervent prayers, not for my safety, because I did not expect any such thing, but for all my past offences; and I may really say I expected my dissolution with a calmness that led me to hope I had made my peace with heaven. At last I fell asleep, though I tried all I could against it, by getting up and walking, till I was obliged, through weariness, to lie down again.

When I awoke in the morning, I was amazed to find myself among four or five very low sandy islands, separated half a mile or more, as I guessed, by the sea. With that I began to be a little cheerful, and walked about to see if I could find any thing that was eatable; but to my great grief I found nothing but a few eggs, which I was obliged to eat raw. The fear of starving seemed to me to be worse than that of drowning; and often did I wish that the sea had swallowed me, rather than thrown me on this desolate island; for I could perceive, by the evenness of them, that they were not inhabited either by man or beast, or any thing else but rats, and several sorts of fowl. Upon this island there were some bushes of a wood they call burton wood, which used to be my shelter at night; but, to complete my misery, there was not to be found one drop of fresh water any where, so that I was forced to drink sea water for two or three days, which made my skin come off like the peel of a broiled codlin. At last my misery so increased, that I often was in the mind of terminating my life, but desisted, from the expectation I had that some alligator, or other voracious creature, would come and do it for me.

I had lived a week upon eggs only, when, by good fortune, I discovered a bird called a booby sitting upon a bush. I ran immediately, as fast as I could, and knocked it down with a stick. I never considered whether it was proper food, but sucked the blood and ate the flesh with such a pleasure as none can express but those who have felt the pain of hunger to the same degree as myself. After I had devoured this banquet, I walked about and discovered many more of these birds, which I killed. My stomach being now pretty well appeased, I began to consider whether I could not with two sticks make a fire as I had seen the blacks do in Jamaica. I tried with all the wood I could get, and at last happily accomplished it. This done, I gathered some more sticks, and made a fire, picked several of my boobies, and broiled them as well as I could; and now I resolved to come to an allowance.

At night, I and my fellow inhabitants endured a great storm of rain and thunder, with the reddest lightning I had ever seen, which well washed us all I believe. As for myself, my clothes, which were only a pair of thin shoes and thread stockings, and a canvass waistcoat and trousers, were soundly wet; but I had the happiness to find in the morning several cavities of rain water, which put in my head a thought of making a deep well, or hollow place, that I might have water continually by me, which I brought to perfection in this manner: I took a piece of wood, and pitched upon a place under a burton tree, where, with my hands and the stick together, I dug a hole, or well, big enough to contain a hogshead of water; then I put in stones and paved it, and got in and stamped them down hard all round, and, with my sticks, beat the sides close, so that I made it capable of holding water. But the difficulty was how to get the water there, which I at length effected by means of a sort of bucket made from a part of my clothing. I now felt greatly cheered with my prospects, and thought I should not be very badly off for a while; for besides the water for my drink, I had ready broiled forty boobies, designing to allow myself half a one a-day. I had a small Ovid, printed by Elzevir, which was in my trousers' pocket when I was going up the ladder of ropes; and, by being pressed close, was not quite spoiled but only the cover off, and a little stained with the wet. This was a great mitigation of my misfortune; for I could entertain myself with this book under a burton bush till I fell asleep. I remained always in good health, only a little troubled with the headache, for want of a hat, which I lost in the water, in falling down from the ladder of ropes. But I remedied this as well as I could, by gathering a parcel of chicken weed, which grows there in plenty, and strewing it over the burton bushes under which I sat. Nay, at last, finding my time might be longer there than I expected, I tore off one of the sleeves of my shirt, and lined a cap that I had made of green sprigs, twisted with the green bark that I peeled off.

I had been here a month by my reckoning, and in that time my skin looked as if it had been rubbed over with walnut shells. I several times thought to have swum to one of the other islands; but as they looked only like heaps of sand, I believed I had got the best berth, so contented myself with my present station. Of boobies I could get enough, who built on the ground, and another bird, that lays eggs, which I used to eat, but I never ventured to taste the eggs. I was so well satisfied with my boobies, that I did not care to try experiments. The island which I was upon, seemed to me to be about two miles in circumference, and was almost round. On the west side there is a good anchoring place, for the water is very deep within two fathoms of the shore. God forgive me! but I often wished to have had companions in my misfortune, and hoped every day either to have seen some vessel come that way, or a wreck, where, perhaps, I might have found some necessaries which I wanted. I used to fancy, that if I should be forced to stay there long, I should forget my speech; so I used to talk aloud, ask myself questions, and answer them. But if any body had been by to have heard me, they would certainly have thought me bewitched, I often asked myself such odd questions. All this while I could not inform myself where I was, or how near any inhabited place.

One morning, which I took to be the 8th of November, a violent storm arose, which continued till noon. In the mean time, I discerned a bark labouring with the waves for several hours; and at last, with the violence of the tempest, perfectly thrown out of the water upon the shore, within a quarter of a mile from the place where I observed it. I ran to see if there were any body I could assist, when I found four men (being all there were in the vessel) busy about saving what they could. When I came up with them, and hailed them in English, they seemed mightily surprised; they asked me "how I came there, and how long I had been there."

C

When I told them my story, they were concerned for themselves as well as for me, for they found there was no possibility of getting their bark off the sands, the wind having forced her so far; with that we began to bemoan one another's misfortunes; but I must confess to you, without lying, I was never more rejoiced in my whole life, for they had on board plenty of every thing for a twelvemonth, and not any article spoiled. Their lading (which was logwood) they had thrown overboard, to lighten the ship, which was the occasion of the wind forcing her so far. Had they kept in their lading, they would have bulged in the sands, half a quarter of a mile from the place where they did; and the sea, flying over them, would not only have spoiled their provisions, but perhaps have been the death of them all. By these men I understood to what place I had got, namely, one of the islands of Alcranes, which are five islands, or rather large banks of sand, for there is not a tree or bush upon any but that where we were. They lie in the latitude of twenty-two degrees north, twenty-five leagues from Yucatan, and about sixty from Campeachy town. We worked as fast as we could, and got at every thing that would be useful to us before night. We had six barrels of salt beef, three of pork, two of biscuit, a small copper and iron pot, several wearing clothes, and a spare hat, which I wanted mightily. We had, besides, several cags of rum, and one of brandy, and a chest of sugar, with many other things of use, some gunpowder, and one fowling-piece. We took off the sails from the yards, and, with some pieces of timber, raised a hut big enough to hold twenty men, under which we put their beds that we got from the bark. It is true we had no shelter from the wind, for the trees were so low they were of no use. I now thought myself in a palace, and was as merry as if I had been at Jamaica, or even at home in my own country. In short, when we had been there some time, we began to be very easy, and to wait contentedly till providence should fetch us out of this island. The bark lay upon the sands, fifty yards from the water, when at the highest, so that I used to lie in her cabin, by reason there were no more beds ashore, than were for my four companions, to wit, Thomas Randal of Cork, in Ireland, whose bed was largest, which he did me the favour to spare a part of, now and then, when the wind was high, and I did not care to lie on board; Richard White, William Musgrave of Kingston, in Jamaica, and Ralph Middleton of Cowes, in the Isle of Wight. These men, with eight others, set out of Port Royal about a month after us, bound for the same place; but the latter, lying ashore, and wandering too far up the country, were met, as it is supposed, by some Spaniards and Indians, who set upon them in great numbers. Yet, nevertheless, by all appearance, they fought desperately; for when Mr Randal and Mr Middleton went to seek for them, they found all the eight dead, with fifteen Indians, and two Spaniards. All the Englishmen had several cuts in their heads, arms, breasts, &c. that made it very plainly appear they had sold their lives dearly. They were too far up in the country to bring down their dead, so they were obliged to dig a hole in the earth, and put them in as they lay, in their clothes. As for the Indians and Spaniards, they stripped them, and left them above ground as they found them, and made all the haste they could to embark, for fear of any other unlucky accident that might happen. They set sail as soon as ever they came on board, and made the best of their way for Jamaica, till they were overtaken by the storm that shipwrecked them on Make-Shift Island, as I had named it.

Now, we had all manner of fishing-tackle with us, but we wanted a boat to go a little way from shore to catch fish; therefore we set our wits to work, in order to make some manner of float, and at last we pitched upon this odd project: we took six casks, and tarred them all over, then stopped up the bungs with corks, and nailed them close down with a piece of tarred canvass. These six casks we tied together with some of the cordage of the vessel, and upon them we placed the skuttles of the deck, and fixed them, and made it so strong, that two men might sit upon them; but for fear a storm should happen, we tied to one end of her a coil or two of small rope, of five hundred fathoms long, which we fixed to a small stake on the shore. Then two of them went out (as for my part I was no fisherman) in order to see what success they should have, but returned with only one nurse, a fish so called, about two feet long, something like a shark, only its skin is very rough, and, when dry, will do the same office as a seal skin. The same, boiled in lemon juice, is the only remedy in the world for the scurvy, by applying pieces of the skin to the calves of your legs, and rubbing your body with some of the liquor once or twice. We sent out our fishermen the next day again, and they returned with two old wives, and a young shark, about two feet long, which were dressed for dinner, and they proved excellent eating. In the morning following we killed a young seal with our fowling-pieces. This we salted, and it ate very well, after lying two or three days in the brine.

We passed our time in this Make-Shift Island as well as we could, and invented several games to divert ourselves. One day, when we had been merry, sorrow, as after gaiety often happens, stole insensibly on us all. I, as being the youngest, began to reflect on my sad condition, spending my youth on a barren land, without hopes of being ever redeemed. Whereupon, Mr Randal, who was a man of great experience, and had come through many sufferings, gave me considerable comfort in my affliction, both by a narrative of his own mishaps, and by a plan he laid before us of a means of getting off the island. " Mr Falconer, and my fellow sufferers," said he, " but it is you," pointing at me, " that I chiefly address myself, as you seem to despair of a safe removal from this place more than any other. Is not your condition much better now than you could have expected it to be a month ago? There is a virtue in manly suffering; as, to repine, seems to doubt of the all-seeing Power which regulates our actions. Our bark is strong and firm; and, by degrees, I do not doubt, but with time and much labour, to get her into the water again. I have been aboard her this morning, when you were all asleep, and examined her carefully, inside and out, and fancy our liberty may soon be effected. I only wonder we have never thought before of clearing the sand from our vessel, which, once done, I believe we may launch her out into deep water."

Having spent the night in reflection on what had passed, the next morning we went to work to clear the sand from our vessel, which we continued working on for sixteen days together, resting only on Sunday, which at last we effected. The next thing we had to do was to get poles to put under our vessel to launch her out; which we got from the burton wood, but with much difficulty, as we were forced to cut a great many, before we could get them that were fit for our purpose. After we had done this, we returned God thanks for our success hitherto; and, on the day following, resolved to thrust off our vessel into the water, but we were prevented by Mr Randal being taken ill of a fever, occasioned, as we supposed, by his great fatigue in working to free our ship from the sand, wherein he spared no pains to encourage us, as much by his actions as his words, even beyond his strength. The concern we were all in upon this, occasioned our delay in not getting our vessel out. Besides, one hand out of five was a weakening of our strength. Mr Randal never thought of his instruments till now, when he wanted to let himself blood; but not feeling them about his clothes, we supposed they might have been overlooked in the vessel; so I ran immediately to see if I could find them; and, getting up the side, my very weight pulled her down to the sand, which had certainly bruised me to death if I had not sunk into the hollow that we had made by throwing the sand from the ship. I crept out in a great fright, and ran to my companions, who, with much ado, got her upright; and afterwards we fixed some spare oars on each side to keep her up from falling again, for the pieces of wood that were placed under her were greased, to facilitate her slipping into the water, and we had dug the sand so entirely from her, that she rested only on them, which occasioned her leaning to one side with my weight only. When we were entered into the vessel, and our endeavours to find the box of instruments were fruitless, we were all mightily concerned, for we verily believed that bleeding would have cured him; nay, even he himself said, that if he could be let blood, he was certain his fever would abate, and he should be easier; yet to see with what a perfect resignation he submitted to the will of heaven, would have inspired one with a true knowledge of the state good men enjoy after a dissolution from this painful life. He grew still worse and worse, but yet so patient in his sufferings, that it perfectly amazed us all. He continued in this manner a whole week, at the end of which time he expired. After our sorrow for his death was something abated, we consulted how to bury him, and at last agreed on committing his body to the hole in the sand which I had dug for my well. After fulfilling this melancholy duty, the whole of our thoughts were bent on our vessel, and the means of escape from the island. The narrative of what was effected, must however remain to be told in the Second Part of my Adventures.

Part II.

On Monday, the 31st of December, we launched our vessel out into the sea, and designed to set sail the next day from the island upon which we had been so long confined. After we had fixed her fast with two anchors and a hawser on shore, we went on board to dine and make ourselves merry, which we did very heartily; and, to add to our mirth, we made a large can of punch, which we never attempted to do before, as we had but one bottle of lime juice in all, which was what indeed we designed for this occasion. In short, the punch ran down so merrily, that we were all in a drunken condition. When it was gone, we resolved to go to rest; but all I could do could not persuade them to lie on board that night in their cabins, yet without a bed: they would venture, though they were obliged to swim a hundred yards before they could wade to shore; but however, they got safe, which I knew by their hallooing and rejoicing.

Having brought my bed on board, I went to rest very contentedly, which I did till next morning: but, oh horror! when I had dressed myself, and, going on deck to call my companions to come on board to breakfast, which was intended overnight, and afterwards to go on shore, and bring our sails and yards on board, and make to sea as fast as we could, I could not see any land! which so overcame me on the sudden, that I sank down on the deck, without sense or motion. How long I continued so I cannot tell, but I awoke full of the sense of my melancholy condition; and ten thousand times, in spite of my resolution to forbear, cursed my unhappy fate that had brought me to that deplorable state. Instead of coming on board to be frolicsome and merry, we should have given thanks to Him who gave us the blessing of thinking we were no longer subject to such hardships that we might probably have undergone, if we had been detained longer on that island. I had no compass, neither was I, of myself, capable of ruling the vessel in a calm, much less if there should a storm happen, which are too frequent in this climate.

After I had vented my grief in a torrent of words and tears, I began to think how the vessel could be got to sea without my knowledge. By remembrance of the matter, the night before, I found, by our eagerness and fatal carelessness, we had forgotten to fasten our cables to the geers; and, pulling up the hawser which we had fastened to one of the burton trees on shore, I perceived that the force of the vessel had pulled the tree out of the earth. Then I too late found that a hurricane had risen when I was sound asleep and stupified with too much liquor. When I began to be something better contented in my mind, and thought of sustaining nature, almost spent with fatigue and grieving, one great comfort I had on my side, which my poor wretched companions wanted, was provision in plenty, and fresh water; so that when I began to consider coolly, I found I had not that cause to complain which they had, who were left on a barren island, without any other provision than that very same diet which I was forced to take up with when first thrown on shore.

I remained tossed upon the sea for a fortnight, without discovering land; for the weather continued very calm, but yet so hazy that I could not perceive the sun for several days. One day, searching for some linen that I had dropped under the sacking of my bed, for I did not lie in a hammock, I found a glove with seventy-five pieces of eight in it, which I took, and sewed in the waistband of my trousers, for fear I should want it some time or other. I made no scruple in taking it, for I was well assured it had belonged to poor Mr Randal. Besides, I had heard the other people say that they were sure that he had money somewhere; and, after his death, we searched for it, but could not find any. January the 20th, 1700, I discovered a sail near me, but she bore away so fast, that there was not any hope of succour from her, and I had not any thing to distinguish me. I supposed, though I could see them, yet they could not see me, by reason of my want of sail, which would have made me the more conspicuous. The next day I discovered land, about six leagues to the southwest of me, which I observed; my vessel did not come nigh, but coasted along shore. I was well assured it was the province of Yucatan, belonging to the Spaniards, and was the place we came from. Now, all my fear was that I should fall into their hands, who would make me do the work of a slave; but even that I thought was better than to live in continual fear of storms and tempests, or shipwreck.

I coasted along in this manner for two or three days, and at last discovered land right ahead, which I was very glad of; but yet mixed with fear, in not knowing what treatment I should have. On January the 30th, I made the bay and town of Francisco di Campeachy, as it proved afterwards, and was almost upon it before I was met by any thing of a ship or a boat; but at last two canoes came on board, with one Spaniard and six Indians, who were much surprised when they understood my condition, by speaking broken French, which the Spaniards understood. They immediately carried me on shore, and thence to the governor, who was at dinner. They would have made me stay till he had dined; but he, hearing of me, commanded me to come in where he was at dinner with several gentlemen and two ladies; and though it is very rare any one sees the women, yet they did not offer to veil themselves. I was ordered to sit down by myself at a little table placed for that purpose, where I had sent me of what composed their dinner, which was some fish and fowls, and excellent wine of several sorts.

After they had feasted me for two or three days, they sent me about, with several officers appointed by the governor, to make a gathering, which we did with success, for in three days we had got seven hundred and odd pieces of eight; and two merchants there were at the charge of fitting up my bark, in order to send it for my poor companions, to hearten us up, as some bottles of fine wines, two bottles of citron water for a cordial, chocolate, and several other useful things; but the difficulty was to get seamen to go with me. At last they remembered they had five Englishmen, that were prisoners there, and taken in the Bay of Campeachy upon suspicion of piracy, but nothing could be proved against them, whom they freed without any ransom. I indeed received as much humanity among them as could be expected from any of the most civilised nations.

All things being prepared, on the 15th of February 1700 we set sail from Campeachy Bay, after paying my acknowledgments to the generous governor; but having nothing to present him worth acceptance but my Ovid, I gave him that, which he took very kindly, and said he would prize it mightily, not only in the esteem he had for that author, but in remembrance of me and my misfortunes. We plied it to the windward very briskly, and in fifteen days discovered the isles of the Alcranes; but we durst not go in within the shoals, because we were all ignorant of the channel. So we cast anchor, and hoisted out our boat, with two men and myself, and made to shore, where we found my three companions, but in a miserable condition, and Mr Musgrave so faint and weak, that they expected he could not live long.

They mentioned to me, that when they awaked, after I had drove off in the vessel in the dark from the island, they were all in despair to find the ship gone, which they perceived was occasioned by a hurricane, that they were assured was violent, because it had blown down their tent, though without awaking them. But when they began to consider they had no food, and but very little fresh water, which was left in a barrel without a head in the tent, their despair increased. But as no passion can last long that is violent, it wore off with their care for sustenance, which they diligently searched for; and not finding any quantity of eggs or boobies, the dreadful fear of starving came into their minds, with all its horrid attendants. They had been five days without eating or drinking, for the boobies were retired out of fear or custom to some other place; neither could they find one egg more; and weakness came so fast upon them, with hunger and drought, that they were hardly able to crawl, so they thought of nothing but dying; when, at last, they remembered the body of good Mr Randal, that had been buried a week, which they dug up without being putrified; and that poor wretch, that helped to support our misfortunes when alive with his sage advice, now was a means of preserving their life, though dead. We arrived in time to save them from continuing this horrid cannibalism; and having seen the remains of my old friend once more consigned to the tomb, we all got on board our vessel, in order to sail as soon as the wind would rise, it being stark calm, and continued so two days. At last it blew a little, and we weighed anchor, and stood out to sea, but made but little way. I now was master or captain of a ship, and began to take upon me. We were nine men, all English; that is, myself first, Richard White, W. Musgrave, and Ralph Middleton, my old companions; John Stone, W. Keater, Francis Hood, W. Warren, and Joseph Meadows (all of England), the five men given me by Don Antonio, who, as I said before, were taken on suspicion of piracy. Whereupon a thought came into my head that had escaped me before. I considered if these were really pirates, being five to four, they might be too powerful for us, and perhaps murder us. One day we all dined together upon deck, under our awning, it being very calm weather. I then asked the five men, what was the reason that they were taken by the Spaniards for pirates? Upon this they seemed nonplussed; but Warren soon recovered himself, as well as all the rest, and spake for the others in this manner:—" We embarked on board the ship Bonaventure, in the Thames, bound for Jamaica, whither we made a prosperous voyage; but after taking in our lading, in our way home we were overtaken by a storm, in which our ship was lost, and all the men perished, except myself and four companions, who were saved in the long-boat. But the reason we were taken for pirates was, that making to shore to save ourselves, we saw a bark riding at anchor without the port of Campeachy, which we made to, in order to inquire whereabouts we were, and to beg some provisions, our own being gone. On entering the vessel, we found but two people in it; the third, jumping into the water, swam on shore, and brought three boats filled with Spanish soldiers, which came on board before we could make off." " Make off!" said I; " what! did you design to run away with the vessel?" " No," answered Warren, with some confusion, " but we did design to weigh anchor, and go farther in shore, that we might land in the morning, it being late at night."

I must confess I did not like the fellow being nonplussed now and then, in not knowing what to say, but, upon consideration, thought it might be for want of words to express himself better; so for that time I took no more notice, not weighing it in my mind; but in the evening Mr Middleton came to me, with a face of concern, and told me he did not like these fellows' tale. "Why so?" said I. "Because I observe they herd together," answered he, "and are always whispering and speaking low to one another. If a foreboding heart may speak, I am sure we shall suffer something from these fellows that will be of danger to us."

Upon this I began to stagger in my opinion of their honesty, and therefore we resolved to stand upon our guard. We took no notice of our conference then to our two other companions, but resolved to stay till night, having a better opportunity then, as we lay together in the cabin aft. When we were to go to supper, we called one another to come; but five of the sailors excused themselves by saying they had dined so lately that they had no stomach as yet; whereupon we had an opportunity sooner to converse together than we designed; for, being at supper, we opened the matter to our other two companions, and they agreed immediately that we were in some danger; so we resolved in the middle watch of the night to seize them in their sleep. We were to have the first watch, which we set at eight o'clock; then they were to watch till twelve; and then, in the third watch, between one and two, we had concluded to seize upon them as they slept; that is, four of them, for one of them watched with us, which was Frank Hood, the cook, whom we agreed to seize and bind fast, towards the latter end of the watch, and to threaten him with death if he offered to make the least noise.

As soon as ever our first watch was set, we sent Mr Musgrave to prepare our arms. In about half an hour, or thereabouts, Warren called to Hood upon deck (they lying below), to get him a little water, "for he was very dry," he said: whereupon, the other went down immediately with some water in a can to him. As soon as he was gone down, I had the curiosity to draw as near the scuttle as I could, to hear the discourse. Now, you must know, Hood, our cook, had been employed that day about searching our provisions, our beef casks and pork, to see what quantity we had, that we might know how long it would last; so that the others had not an opportunity to disclose the design to him. As soon as he was got down, I could hear Will Warren say to him, "Hark ye, Frank, we had like to have been smoked to-day; and though we had contrived the story that I told you, yet I was a little surprised at their asking me, because then I did not expect it; but we design to be even with them in a very little time; for hark ye—" said he, and spoke so low that I could not hear him: upon which the other said, "There is no difficulty in the matter; but we need not be in such haste, for you know, as we ply it to windward, a day or two can break no squares, and we can soon (after the effecting our design) bear down to leeward to our comrades, that we left on shore; for I fancy," added he, "that they have some small suspicion of you now, which in time will sleep, and may be on their guard; therefore it is better to wait a day or two."

"No; we'll do it to-night when they are asleep," replied Warren; whereupon there were many arguments *pro* and *con* as I fancied. A little while after, Hood came up again; and after walking up and down, and fixing his eyes often upon me, who in the meantime was provided with a couple of pistols under my watch-coat, and which, indeed, were their own, that we had hung up, ready charged, in our cabin (which was one reason of their design to attack us in our sleep), Hood, as I said before, seemed to fix his eyes frequently on me, for, till now, I never watched in the night. At last, said he, very softly, "If you please, Mr Falconer, I have a word or two to say to you, that much concerns you all." "What is it?" said I. "Why," answered he, "I would have the rest of your companions ear-witnesses too:" with that I called them together; "but," said he, "let us retire as far from the scuttle as we can, that we may not be heard by any below deck;" so we went into the cabin, and opened the scuttle above, that Mr Musgrave, who steered, might hear what was said. When we had sat down upon the floor,

Hood began as follows:—"My four companions below have a wicked design upon you; that is to seize you, and put you into the boat, and run away with the vessel; but I think it is an inhuman action, not only to any one, but to you in particular, that have been the means of their freedom." Upon this (finding his sincerity), I told him that we were provided against it already; and, with the consent of my companions, I told him of our design of seizing them in the third watch. "But," said he, "they intend to put their project in practice their next watch; therefore I think 'twill be more proper for us to counterplot them and seize them this." "As they have no arms," said I, "and we have, we need not fear them."

We had several debates about this, which took up too much time, to our sorrow; for Warren, mistrusting Hood, it seems, got up and listened; and when he found that we retired, all of us, to the cabin, he got upon deck, and, stealing softly, came so close that he overheard every thing we said, which, as soon as he understood, he went immediately to his companions, who waited impatiently, as they told us afterwards, and let them know all our discourse; whereupon, without pausing, they resolved to attack us immediately, in the midst of our consultation; which was no sooner resolved upon than done. For we were immediately surprised with their seizing us, which they did with that quickness, and so unperceivable, that we were all confounded and amazed: they had got off two pistols in our consternation, which they clapped to our breasts. In this confusion I had forgotten mine, that were at my girdle (or else we might have been hard enough for them); neither did I remember them till they found them about me. They shut the cabin door on the inside till they had bound us, and never minded Mr Musgrave's knocking and making a noise, till they had secured us; which done, they opened the door and seized him, who came to know what the matter was, for we had no candle in the cabin; and he, hearing a noise amongst us, thought we were seizing Hood, and called to us to forbear (as he afterwards said), and make haste, for he was going to tack about, though we did not hear him; on which, he clapped the helm a-lee, and came down to fetch us out to haul off the sheets, &c., and was seized; and the sails fluttered in the wind, by reason she was veering round when the helm was a-lee.

After they had fixed the vessel, and it was broad day, they came and unbound our legs, and gave us leave to walk upon deck: whereupon I began to expostulate with them, particularly Warren, as he seemed to have a sort of command over the others. "And what," said I to him, " do you design to do with us, now you have your desire?" "Do with you! why, by and bye we design to put you into the boat, and turn you adrift; but, for that Hood, we'll murder him without mercy! A dog, to betray us! but as you have not so much injured us, we'll put you immediately into the boat, with a week's provision, and a small sail, and you shall seek your fortune, as I suppose you would have done by us." "No," answered I; "we only designed to confine you till we came to Jamaica, and there to have given you your liberty to go where you had thought fit: put us ashore at any land that belongs to the English, and we will think you have not done us an injury." "No," said he; "we must go to meet our captain and fifty men, upon the mainland of Yucatan, where our vessel was stranded, not to be gotten off. Our first design, when we were taken in our boat, was to get us a vessel to go a-buccaneering, which we had done at Campeachy, if it had not been for the Indian that swam on shore, unknown to us, and brought succours too soon."

When they had got every thing ready, that is to say, a barrel of biscuit, another of water, about half a dozen pieces of beef, and as much pork, a small kettle, and a tinder-box, we were better provided than we expected, by much: besides, they granted us four cutlasses, and a fowling-piece, with about four pounds of powder and a sufficient quantity of shot; together with all poor Mr Randal's journals, after their perusing them and finding them of no use. When this was done, Warren ordered them to tie Hood to the mast of the vessel, and was charging a pistol to shoot him through the head, not considering it was charged before; for it was one of them I had at my girdle, and which they took from me, but in his eagerness and heat of passion he did not mind it. We all entreated for the poor fellow, and he himself fell upon his knees, and begged, with all the eloquence he had, to spare him, and let him go with us; but Warren swore bitterly nothing could save him: with that he cocked his pistol and levelled it at Hood, but firing, it split into several pieces, and one struck Warren, into the skull, so deep, that he was breathing his last upon deck. One of the bullets grazed upon the side of my temple, and did but just break the skin: as for Hood, he was not hurt; but with the fright, and noise of the pistol (as we supposed), laboured with such an agony of spirit, that he broke the cords that tied him by the arms, though as thick as a middle finger, and fell down, but rose immediately; and, not finding himself hurt, ran to us, and unbound our arms, unperceived by the other two, who were busy about the unfortunate Warren; and though they were called to, by them that steered (who ran immediately to prevent it), yet they did not mind it, they were so concerned about Warren. Before he that steered came, Hood had unbound me, and stopped the fellow (Meadows) by giving him a blow with his fist that knocked him down. In the meantime, I had unbound White, Musgrave, and Middleton, and we went and seized upon the other two pirates, as now we called them nothing else.

After we had bound them in our turn, we went to see what assistance could be given to Warren, when we found that a piece of the barrel of the pistol had sunk into his skull, and that he was just expiring; but yet he sat up with great resolution. " You have overpowered us," said he, " and I likewise see the hand of heaven is in it. I was born of good honest parents, whose steps, if I had followed, would have made my conscience easy to me at this time; but I forsook all religion, and now, too late, I find that to dally with

Heaven is fooling one's self: but yet, in this one moment of my life that is left, I heartily repent of all my past crimes, and rely upon the Saviour of the world, that died for our sins, to pardon mine." With that he crossed himself and expired. I must confess I was very sorry for the unhappy accident of his death, but yet glad that we were at liberty, and felt something easy that the poor soul repented before his expiring.

After we had secured our Tartars, we threw Warren overboard, and bore to the wind; for after our first tacking about in the morning, when the bustle happened, they bore away with tack at cat-head, as being for their purpose. The three men that were left, desired us to let them have the boat, and go seek their companions, which we refused, not having hands enough to carry our vessel to Jamaica. But we promised them, if they would freely work in the voyage, they should have their entire liberty to go where they thought fit, without any complaints against them. Upon this, we began to be a little sociable, as before; and they all declared, that what they did was at the instigation of Warren.

The next day we discovered a ship to windward of us, that bore down upon us with crowded sails. We filled all the sails we had, and endeavoured to get away from her as fast as we could, but all to no purpose. We saw they gained upon us every moment; and therefore seeing it was not possible for us to escape, we backed our sails, and lay by for them, that they might be more civil if they were enemies. As soon as ever they came up with us, they hailed us, and ordered us to come on board, which we durst not deny, when Mr Musgrave and I, with Hood and White, for rowers, went on board them. We found by Hood's knowing that they were his captain and comrades. Now, as Hood said, we did not know how we should behave ourselves, or what we should say about Warren; but we only told the captain how we met with his men, and that they were redeemed upon my account. He never asked particularly for Warren, but how they all did; and when they sent on board to search our vessel, they soon came to the truth,

D

for the other three told them the story, though not with aggravated circumstances, upon which, poor Hood was tied to the main-mast, lashed with a cat-o'-nine-tails, most abominably, and after that pickled in brine, which was more pain than the whipping; but it kept his back from festering, which it might otherwise have done, because they flay the skin at every stroke, and then wash it with brine, which is called whipping and tickling. After this, they would not keep him among them, but sent for the other three men from our vessel, and ordered us all on board, with another of their men, who was ill of a dangerous fever, which they feared might prove infectious. They did not take any thing from us, as we expected at first; only gave us this sick man to look after, which we were very contented with; so we parted with them very well satisfied, but much better when we were out of sight, fearing they had forgotten themselves, and would send for us back, and take our provisions from us, or one mischief or another; for pirates do not often use to be so courteous.

PART III.

Two nights after we had parted from the pirate, we encountered a dreadful storm, that lasted two days without abating; and our poor bark, which was none of the best, was tumbled and tossed about like a tennis ball, yet we received no damage, but that she would not answer the helm; so we were obliged to let her go before the tempest, and trust to the mercy of heaven for relief. We in the middle of the storm discovered land right ahead, which put us all into our panics. We endeavoured to bring our vessel to bear up to the wind, but all to no purpose, for she still drove nearer the shore, where we discovered several tokens of a shipwreck, as pieces of broken masts, and barrels swimming on the water, and a little farther, men's hats. Then we began to think that we certainly should run the same fate—when, as soon as thought, our bark was driven on shore in a smooth sandy bay, where we had opportunity to quit her, which was happy for us, for the sea washed over her with such violence, that we had not any hopes of her escaping the storm, and thought, of course, we should be torn to pieces.

When we were ashore, we all concluded it could be no other land but the south of Cuba island, belonging to the Spaniards. We were then in a terrible fright lest we were near any place that belonged to the Indians; for Musgrave assured me that there were some parts of the south side of Cuba, that Indians dwelt in, in spite of the Spaniards, and massacred them, wherever they met with them, or any other whites. We remained all night in great fear; and though we found the storm abated, or rather a calm succeeded, yet we durst not stir till the moon rose, and then we walked towards our vessel, which we found all on one side; but, by good fortune, most of our provisions were dry, which mightily rejoiced us. But all the vessel's rigging and masts were shattered and torn to pieces, and some part of her quarter wrung off, so that she could not be of any use to us if we could have got her upright. We took out all our provision, and our arms, with two barrels of gunpowder, that were dry, the rest being damaged with water and sand that had got in. We had arms enough, as having those that belonged to the three sailors that were taken in the pirate, which we supposed they had forgotten; so we were six men well armed, with each a musket, a case of pistols, and a bayonet, besides two cutlasses, if we should need them. By the time we had taken every thing out, day approached, and then we designed, altogether, well armed, to go and view the country. John Rouse was very well recovered of his fever, but a little weak; yet his heart was as good as the best of us; so we resolved, if we were set upon by Indians, to defend ourselves to the last drop of blood, choosing rather to die by their hands in fight, than to be tortured after their usual manner.

When we had placed our provision, and other necessaries, safe behind a tuft of trees, that grew close by the water-side, we fixed our arms, and ventured to walk up in the country, which we did almost every way that day, four or five miles, but could not discover any living creature, nor any sign of inhabitants; only in one place the grass seemed to be lately trodden, but whether by man or beast we could not discover; so, being tired, we went back again to our station, where we ate heartily, and at night we laid ourselves upon the grass, and fell asleep, for we durst not lie upon the sails we had got for that purpose, as they were not dry, though spread all day long.

I was awakened the next morning by a company of lizards creeping over me, which is an animal frightful enough to look at, but very harmless, and great lovers of mankind. They say that these creatures (if any person lie asleep, and any voracious beast, or the alligator, which comes on shore often, is approaching the place where you lie) will crawl to you as fast as they can, and, with their forked tongues, tickle you till you awake, that you may avoid, by their timely notice, the coming danger. I got up, being roused by these animals, and looked about me, but saw nothing except an odd kind of a snake, about two feet long, having a head something like a weasel, and eyes fiery like a cat; as soon as it spied me, it ran away, and my dog after it, but he did not kill it.

We now resolved on another walk to discover what inhabitants were our neighbours, whether Indians or Spaniards; if Indians, we designed to patch up our boat, which had several holes in it, and make off as fast as we could, and row northward, till we came to some place inhabited by Spaniards. But if we found the latter, to beg protection, and some means to get to Jamaica, whereupon we ventured out with these resolutions.

We had not gone far before my dog began to bark, when, turning my head on one side, I beheld a black approaching us; and being startled at the sight, I cocked my piece, and resolved to fire at him; but he called to me in English, and told me he did not come to do me any harm, but was a poor distressed Englishman that wanted food and was almost starved, having eaten nothing but wild fruit for four days: upon that I let him come near, when he was soon known by Rouse to be William Plymouth, the black trumpeter to the captain that commanded the pirate ship. Upon this, knowing him, we sat down and gave him some provision, which we had brought with us, because we designed to be out all day.

After he had refreshed himself a little, we asked him how he came into this island? To which he answered, "We were cruising about Cuba, in hopes of some Spanish prize, when a storm arose and drove us upon a rock, where our ship was beaten to pieces, and not above eighteen men saved besides the captain." "And did that wicked wretch escape the shipwreck?" said I. "Yes," answered Plymouth, "but to undergo a more violent death; for as soon as ever we landed, we wandered up in the country to seek for some food, without any weapons but a few cutlasses, having lost our fire-arms; but, however, we all got something or other to defend ourselves on shore, as long clubs, which we took from the trees we found in our walks. Our captain resolved, if he met with any Indian or Spanish huts, he would murder all that he found in them, for fear they should make their escape, and bring more upon us. Thus he encouraged his men to follow him with their clubs: 'We will walk,' said he, 'till we find some beaten path, and there lie hid till night, when we may go on to some house, and come upon them undiscovered, by which means we may get provision and other arms;' for the Indians of Cuba use fire-arms as well as the Spaniards, and are full as dexterous in using them as any Europeans. After travelling about ten miles to the north-west, we discovered a path, upon which a halt was commanded; and we retired into the woods again till night, and dined upon what fruits we could get upon the trees.

About two hours before night a dog smelled us out, and, running away from us, barked most furiously: upon that we were afraid of being discovered, which fear proved true; for in half an hour, or thereabouts, after the dog left us, we were saluted with several arrows and musket shot, that killed three men, and wounded me in the foot; but it proved the means of saving my life; for as soon as our men perceived what had happened, they ran as hard as they could to meet the danger; knowing they could do no good till they came to handy-blows, I, in endeavouring to follow them, found my hurt, which prevented me keeping up with the rest; but I could hear and see them at it. About 200 Indians set upon our men, and in half an hour killed them every one. I saw the captain lay about him desperately, but at last he fell, being run through the throat with a wooden stake. As soon as ever the Indians had conquered, or rather murdered them, they fell to stripping them as fast as they could, and carried them off, together with their own dead, which were many, for the English sold their lives very dearly.

After they were gone, I ventured to steal out from behind a row of bushes, where I had placed myself to see what had happened. I went to the place of battle, where I found two of our men that they had left, with all their arms; so I took up one of their best muskets and a cutlass, and made farther into the wood, for fear of being caught, which I had certainly been, if I had staid a quarter of an hour longer; for I soon heard them hooping, screaming, and hallooing back, to fetch the other two bodies and their arms, as I conjectured.

I walked as far as my injured foot would let me that night, and out of the danger of the Indians, as I thought, and then laid me down to sleep as well as I could, being very hungry, and sadly tired, and slept very well till morning, when I proceeded forward in my painful journey, and directed my course north-east, thinking that was the best way to avoid the Indians, and probably to meet with some Spaniards, who I knew inhabited towards the north; the Havannah, the capital city of the whole island, being seated there. I wandered for four days, eating nothing but fruit in the woods; but laying myself down about an hour ago, to rest myself a little, I thought I heard the tongues of Englishmen, which, to my great joy, proved true. I left my musket behind the bushes, for fear of alarming you; but now, after returning God and you thanks for this timely nourishment, I'll go and fetch it;" which he did; and it might be easily known to be an Indian piece, for they rudely carved it all over with several figures of birds and beasts.

"Now," said I to my companions, " you see the reward of wickedness. The pirate was not suffered to go on long in his crimes; for though justice has leaden feet, yet they always find she has iron hands."

After poor Plymouth had refreshed himself, we set forward, and walked along till we came to a road that seemed to be the main road of the island. Here we consulted what we should do; whether we should go on or return for more provision: we resolved to go a little distance from the road, for fear we should meet with more of the Indians, and run the same fate with the other Englishmen. But Plymouth told us we were a great way from the place where his countrymen were killed (for Plymouth, though born in Guinea, would always call himself an Englishman, being brought over very young); so we resolved, one and all, to venture.

We sent up prayers to the Almighty for our safety, and went on with an idea that we should come off with success; but we had not gone far, when we heard the reports of several muskets, and shouting in a barbarous manner behind us. Looking that way, we saw a mulatto riding as fast as ever his mule could carry him: when he came up to us, he stopped and cried in Spanish, "Make haste! run!—the Indians are coming upon you; they have killed several Spaniards already, and are fighting with them!" Mr Musgrave, who understood Spanish very well, interpreted what he said to us, and asked how far they were off. He answered, "Just by:" and hearing another shout, put spurs to his mule, and left us in an instant. We found, by the shouting and the firing, that they would be immediately upon us; so we retired out of the road to let them pass, and lay down upon our bellies that they might not discover us.

Immediately came by about twenty Spaniards, on horseback, pursued by near a hundred Indians. Just as they came by us, one Spaniard dropped, and crept into a bush on the other side of the road; and presently the Indians followed, shouting in a horrid manner, and overtook the Spaniards again, who being very swift on foot, outran an ordinary horse; and they had thrown away their fire-arms, to make them the lighter to run, as we supposed. The Spaniards knew they would soon overtake them, so only ran to charge their pistols, and staid till they came up; then discharged them, to put them in confusion, and then ran again to prolong the time, in hopes of some aid. All this we understood by the Spaniard, who crept into the bush undiscovered by the Indians, he being the foremost in flight. He told us, moreover, that about three leagues farther there was a fort belonging to the Spaniards, to stop the Indians, they using to make inroads before that fort was built, even to the gates of the city of Havannah. Upon this we consulted, and resolved to follow on the edge of the road, to see if we could be useful. We soon came even with them, for they were in a narrow place, and the Spaniards kept them at bay pretty well. By good fortune, there was a high hedge, made by trees, all along as we went, which hindered us from being discovered. Here we resolved to fire upon them, altogether, and then run farther up, and, if possible, get out into the road, and face them.

Accordingly, we agreed to fire, four and three, and the first four to charge again immediately. Mr Musgrave, Mr Middleton, Mr White, and myself, agreed to fire first; then Hood, Rouse, and Plymouth; which, as soon as we had taken good aim, we did; and, firing at their backs, killed four downright, and wounded several; for I had ordered them to put two bullets into each piece. As soon as ever we had fired our muskets, we let fly one pistol each, and then the other three fired their guns. After a good deal of fighting and skirmishing, we put the savages completely to the rout. However, we took four of them prisoners, and tying their hands behind them, fastened them to two of our foremost horses, the rest following after, that they might not get loose.

We were met on the road by twenty Spanish horse, with each a foot soldier behind them, who were upon the full gallop to our assistance, having been alarmed by the mulatto that rode by; but I believe some were glad they came too late. The officers and the rest saluted us very courteously, when they heard how luckily we came to their assistance; but they fell a-whipping the poor naked Indians so barbarously, that though they deserved it, I could not bear to see it done; and though the blood followed every lash, yet they never cried out.

We were well entertained at a gentleman's house at dinner, with provision dressed after the English way, and all manner of sweetmeats, and cool wines. As soon as we had dined, we were obliged to get on horseback, and away for the Havannah, which we reached about six o'clock in the evening. We had rooms allotted us; and several Englishmen and Irishmen came to see us who lived there.

I met there with a priest, who I am sure harboured nothing of cruelty in his breast, for he came to see us every day, and in such a friendly manner that charmed us all. He was always sending us one good thing or other, and would take us to divert us abroad. He understood Latin very well, and some English. On the Sunday he preached an excellent sermon in Spanish, in order to excite charity in the auditors, and let us have what was necessary for carrying us to Jamaica. The next day he brought us to the value of L.50 in Spanish dollars, which were collected at the church doors for us. There was a small vessel upon the stocks, that was bought of the owners for us, and a collection made in the town for money to pay for it. This was very agreeable news, and we were told our vessel was ready, and therefore might be going when we pleased. It was a very neat one as ever was built by the Spaniards, and carried between thirteen and fourteen tons. We had all sorts of provision sent on board for half a year, or more; so that we only staid for the wind to rise, it being quite a calm. While we remained there, the four unfortunate Indians were executed in the midst of the parade.

When all was over, Father Antonio took us home to his lodgings, to give us a small collation for the last time, as the next day we all designed to lie on board, in expectation of the wind rising. In the morning we paid our hearty acknowledgments to all our benefactors, and went on board; where we had not been a quarter of an hour before an extraordinary message came from the governor for Plymouth, our black, who went with them without any hesitation, and returned with a present from the governor of several bottles of rack, Spanish wines, fowls, rice, and brandy, with twenty pieces of Spanish gold, as the messenger told us, in recompence for the loss of our companion; for the governor had sent for Plymouth to know if he would serve him in quality of his trumpeter, and a pension should be settled on him for life. Plymouth thought fit to accept of it, as having no master, nor knowing when he should have one; but he got leave to come on board to bid us farewell, which he did in a very affectionate manner; so we parted with Plymouth, and with hearty thanks recommended to father Antonio for all his favours. Plymouth had a trumpet given him by the governor as soon as he came on shore, which he brought with him, and so sounded all the way in the boat, as he went back again, to oblige us, for really he sounded extraordinary well, and had learned on several other instruments, having a tolerable understanding in music. The wind rising, we weighed anchor, and left port with three huzzas, and a volley of small arms (having no cannon), and in two days lost sight of the island of Cuba.

The weather continued favourable, so that we arrived at Jamaica without meeting any thing remarkable in our passage. As soon as we had cast anchor, I ordered the boat to be made ready to carry me on board my own ship, which I saw riding there. But when I got up the ship's side, I found my clothes selling at the mast, at "Who bids more?" which is the method as soon as a person is dead or killed; the first harbour they anchor in, the clothes of the deceased are brought upon the deck and sold by auction; the money to be paid when they come to England; for it generally happens that sailors have not any till they come home again.

They were at the last article when I came up to the ship's side, which was a pair of black worsted stockings, that cost, I believe, about 4s., which went off at 12s. 6d., though they had been worn. As soon as I was seen by them, some cried out, "A ghost! a ghost!" and others ran away to secure the clothes they had bought, suspecting that now I would have them again. When they were satisfied of my being alive, and were told my story, they were all rejoiced at my good fortune, but none could be prevailed upon to let me have my clothes again, so I took up the slop-book, and cast up what they were sold for, and found what cost me about L.20 were sold for four times the money. When I was satisfied in that, I called every person, one by one, that had bought any of my clothes, and struck a bargain with them for ready money, and bought them for about ten pounds; but the ready money pleased them mightily.

Captain Wise being sick ashore, I went to pay him a visit, where he was mighty glad to see me, believing that I had perished. He told me that the vessel hung lights out for several hours, that I might know where to swim, and laid by as long as the wind would permit; as the crew acquainted him when they came into harbour. The captain told me that he did not think he should live long, therefore was extremely glad I was come to take charge of the ship, which would have sailed before if she had been in a condition to bear the sea. From thence I went on board my new bark, and settled my affairs there with my new companions, who were very sorry to think of parting from me. Hood and Rouse desired they might be received on board as sailors, and go to England with us; for Hood was an

Englishman, and Rouse had friends there. Besides, it was as easy to go from England to Bermudas, as from Jamaica. So I spoke to the captain, who was very well pleased to receive them, as he had lost five men by the distemper of the country. Captain Wise died in a week after my coming, and left me executor for his wife, who lived at Bristol.

As soon as we had buried him, I went on board with my two men, designing to sail in three days at farthest, which I would have done before, but that I was hindered by wanting a chapman for our bark, as we had shares to dispose of. When I came on board, the master told me he had no occasion for the two men, to add to their charge. " That is as I shall think fit," said I ; " for the power is in my hands now." " And who put that power into your hands?" said the master. " He that had power so to do," said I; "the captain," whereupon I showed him in writing. He told me "it did not signify any thing, and that he should find no one of the sailors would obey a boy, incapable to steer a vessel. It would be a fine thing," added he, " for my mate to become my captain ; and as I was designed by the captain to have the command of the vessel before you came, so I intend to keep it." "But," said I, "this paper, signed by his own hand, is but of two days' date, and you cannot show any thing for the command, as you pretend to ; therefore I'll make my complaint to the governor, and he shall right me." " Ay, ay, do so," said he ; " I'll stand to any thing he shall command."

Whereupon, Rouse, Hood, and myself, went into the boat again, and rowed immediately on shore ; but the governor was six miles up the country ; and as it was pretty late, we designed to wait for his coming home, which, we were told, would be in the morning early: so I went on board the bark, and lay there all night, the ship lying beyond the quays, two leagues from the harbour, in order to sail. The next morning, getting up with an intent to wait upon the governor, and looking towards the place where the ship lay overnight, I found she was gone ; and casting my eyes towards the sea, saw a ship four or five leagues distant from us, which we supposed to be ours. I immediately went on shore, and found the governor had just come to town, and made my complaint. He told me there was no remedy, but to send immediately to Blewfield's Bay, where he supposed they would stop to get wood, which was usual with our ships that were bound for England: whereupon, there was a messenger ordered for Blewfields, whom I accompanied, to give instructions to the officer that commanded at the fort to seize the master of the ship, and order him before the governor at Port Royal: so we got on horseback, and reached it in three days, it being almost a hundred miles. When we came there, we found several ships in the harbour, but none that we wanted; so we waited a week, all to no purpose; for she passed the bay as mistrusting our design. Upon this we were obliged to return, with heavy hearts, and tell the governor of our ill success, who pitied me, and told me he would see me shipped in the first vessel bound for England: so I went on board my own bark, where they were all glad to see me, though sorry I was so disappointed. Now, I was very glad that I had not disposed of my bark, for I thought it might be of use to me. We consulted together to know what was best to do; at last I made a bargain with them, if they would venture with me in our bark to England. Upon this we agreed; and, with what money I had, I began to load my vessel with things to traffic with. I bought a good quantity of indigo, some cotton, sugar, and rum. In short, I laid out the best part of my money; and on the 1st of June 1700, set sail with a fair wind, and steered our course to England.

We put in at Blewfield's Bay, for the conveniency of obtaining wood and water, and when we were provided, steered our course onward as fast as possible; but as soon as we came within ten leagues of the Havannah, a Spanish man-of-war of forty guns came up with us, and commanded us to strike our sails, which we did immediately; and coming on board us, were surprised to find us all Englishmen, not expecting other than

Spaniards, from the build of our vessel: whereupon they made us all prisoners, and sent fifteen men on board us to carry the vessel into the Havannah; telling them how we came by the vessel did not signify any thing, for they said we were pirates, and had seized it; and our pass, which we had from the governor of Havannah, not being to be found, made things appear so different to what they really were, that it had on the face of it a very suspicious appearance. We were very much afraid we should find a great number of difficulties in obtaining our liberty, especially if they proceeded to their station, which was St Jago. But it happened much better than we had any reason to expect; for she proceeded directly to the Havannah, where we knew every thing would be placed in a true light again. When we were anchored, and the people could come on board us, we were soon known, and the captain, going to the governor, was informed of the matter; so we were released immediately, and had a visit made us from father Antonio and honest Plymouth, who were mightily rejoiced to see us. We were detained two days before we could get away; and then we set sail with a brisk gale, first saluting the town.

In two days after our sailing, we made Cape Florida, and entered the gulf which bears the same name, and passed it without danger. But here a sudden calm overtook us, as frequently happens, when you are past the gulf, and the current set strong to westward, occasioned, as we supposed, by the opening of the land upon that coast. The calm lasting for four days, we were insensibly carried within half a league of the shore; but a little breeze rising from land, helped us farther out again. Still our danger increased; for we soon saw three canoes making towards us, full of armed Indians.

We had not much time to consult what to do, for they gained upon us every moment. Now, death, or something worse than death, stared us in the face; and most of us thought this the last day we had to live. "Come, friends," said I, "if we must die, let us die bravely, like Englishmen." We charged our four guns with double and round, and our patteraroes with musket-balls: the rest of our arms we got in readiness, and resolved to die fighting, and not suffer ourselves to be taken, to be miserably butchered, as all the Indians of Florida do when they get any whites in their power. We resolved to fire our six muskets upon them, as soon as they came within reach; so we took our aim, two at each canoe, and fired upon them, which did them some damage, for they stopped upon it. Whereupon we made the best of our way, but they soon pursued us with loud and rude shouts.

By this time we had charged our pieces the third time, which we fired as before, but did more execution, as they were nearer to us; and now we charged them the fourth time, and laid them along upon the deck for a further occasion.

Looking towards the shore, we saw eight more of their canoes standing towards us. This put us upon making all the sail we could; and the sea-breeze being now pretty strong, we had good way. Being anxious to avoid killing the poor and ignorant creatures, we made all the sail we could, and as they could not keep up with us, we soon left them far behind. And so we sailed on with a prosperous gale, and met with no incident worth recording, till Thursday, the fifteenth of July, when we discovered land, which amazed us all, for we did not think of falling in with any land till we saw England. We went to consult our charts, and saw we were near Newfoundland: and finding that we steered directly into St John's harbour, which is the most commodious in the island, and capital of that part of Newfoundland which belongs to the English, we were very well pleased.

After being there two days, we set sail, and made our course to England, July 25th, 1700. We met with no extraordinary accident in our passage, till we discovered the Land's End, on the 21st of August. How rejoiced I was to see my native country, let them judge that have been placed in the same condition that I have. I may with truth say, that the transports I felt, on first seeing the white cliffs of the island that gave me birth, exceeded the joy I received when I was delivered from the most imminent danger.

THE SOUTH SEA MARAUDERS.

It used to be a common phrase among the most roving and wild class of sailors, " that there was no peace south of the Line." This was certainly the case during the chief part of the sixteenth and seventeenth centuries, when the tropical regions of the west were so dreadfully infested by buccaneers or pirates. These desperadoes belonged to mostly all European nations, but were chiefly English, Dutch, and French, and the whole burden of their cruelty and rapacity fell upon the Spaniards. Against the " Dons," as they called them, they waged a continual war, and, as it appeared, on the specious pretence of revenging the cruelties which the Spanish nation had committed upon the Indians. So much did the Spaniards suffer in this way, that they at length adopted the inglorious expedient of desisting from carrying on an intercourse with their South American colonies. This, however, served but to excite instead of allaying the plundering propensities of the buccaneers, who now landed from their ships and attacked the colonists in their cities. Curiously enough, these depredations met with little attention in England, or in any country to which the pirates belonged. At this period, the English and other courts of Europe generally winked at the evil deeds of the buccaneers, except when pressed to convict and punish them for their murders and robberies on the high seas. So far as the English were concerned in these enterprises, there can be little reason to doubt that the antipathy which both the nation and the government had to the Spaniards—an antipathy originating, in a great measure, in the attempt of the Spanish Armada on the country, in Queen Elizabeth's time, and which lasted even up till the middle of last century—was one of the prevailing causes of the piratical aggressions, and the impunity with which they were committed.

One of the most audacious piratical leaders about the middle of the seventeenth century was Henry Morgan, a Welshman, who contrived to gain the favour and patronage of Charles II. Morgan levied war on his own account, and that of his companions, on a great scale. In 1670, he undertook a grand expedition against the Spanish South American colonies, with thirty-seven sail of vessels and two thousand men, the vessels being well provisioned, and the crews armed to the teeth. After holding a council of war at Cape Tiberoon, it was determined to proceed to attack and plunder the rich town of Panama. But this city was situated on the Pacific side of the South American continent, and the vessels of the pirates were in the Atlantic. It was hence proposed to leave the ships on the coast, and march overland to the place of meditated destruction. The daring project, which would have daunted less resolute men, was instantly put in execution. Morgan landed at Fort San Lorenzo, on the West India side of the isthmus of Darien. Having captured this stronghold, in which he left a garrison of five hundred of his men, and having committed the charge of the ships to a hundred and fifty more, the advance towards the shores of the Pacific was commenced. At first the party ascended the river Chagre in canoes, which took them a certain length. After surmounting incredible difficulties, both on the river and on land, and enduring dreadful fatigue in carrying along their artillery over huge mountains, as well as suffering from famine, they at length, on the ninth day, saw the expanse of the Pacific or South Sea spread out before them. As evening approached, they came in sight of the church towers of Panama, when they halted, and waited impatiently for the morrow. At this period, Panama consisted of seven thousand houses, and was a place of considerable magnificence and wealth.

When the buccaneers resumed their march at an early hour next morning, the Spaniards at once guessed their desperate intentions, and determined on giving them battle. They marched out from the city to meet them, preceded by herds of wild bulls, which they drove upon the adventurers to disorder their ranks. But the buccaneers, as hunters of these wild animals, were too well acquainted with their habits to be discomposed by them; and this attack of the van does not seem to have had much effect. The Spaniards, however, must have made an obstinate resistance, for it was night before they gave way, and the buccaneers became masters of the city. During the long battle, and indeed all that day and night, the buccaneers gave no quarter. Six hundred Spaniards fell. The loss of the buccaneers is not specified, but it appears to have been very considerable.

When master of the city, Morgan was afraid that his men might get drunk, and be surprised and cut off by the Spaniards: to prevent this, he caused it to be reported that all the wine in the city had been expressly poisoned by the inhabitants. The dread of poison kept the fellows sober. But Morgan had scarcely taken up his quarters in Panama when several parts of the city burst out into flames, which, fed by the cedar wood and other combustible materials of which the houses were chiefly built, spread so rapidly, that in a short time a great part of the city was burnt to the ground. It has been disputed whether this was done by design or accident—by the buccaneers or the despairing Spaniards; but it appears that Morgan, who always charged it upon the Spaniards, gave all the assistance he could to such of the inhabitants as endeavoured to stop the progress of the fire, which, however, was not quite extinguished for weeks. Among the buildings destroyed, was a factory-house belonging to the Genoese, who then carried on the trade of supplying the Spaniards with slaves from Africa.

The licentiousness, rapacity, and cruelty of the buccaneers, had no bounds. They spared in these, their cruelties, no sex or condition whatsoever. As to religious persons (monks and nuns) and priests, they granted them less quarter than others, unless they procured a considerable sum of money for their ransom. Detachments scoured the country to plunder and to bring in prisoners. Many of the unfortunate inhabitants escaped, with their effects, by sea, and reached the islands that are thickly clustered in the bay of Panama. But Morgan found a large boat lying aground in the port, which he launched, and manned with a numerous crew, and sent her to cruise among those islands. A galleon, on board which the nuns of a convent had taken refuge, and where much money, plate, and other effects of value, had been lodged, had a very narrow escape from these desperadoes. They took several vessels in the bay. One of them was large, and admirably adapted for cruising. This opened a new prospect that was brilliant and enticing; an unexplored ocean studded with islands was before them, and some of the buccaneers began to consult how they might leave their chief, Morgan, and try their fortunes on the South Sea, whence they proposed to sail, with the plunder they should obtain, by the East Indies to Europe. This diminution of force would have been fatal to Morgan, who, therefore, as soon as he got a hint of the design, cut away the masts of the ship, and burned every boat and vessel lying at Panama that could suit their purpose.

At length, on the 24th of February 1672, about four weeks after the taking of Panama, Morgan and his men departed from the still smouldering ruins of that unfortunate city, taking with them 175 mules loaded with spoil, and 600 prisoners, part of whom were detained to carry burdens across the isthmus, and others for the ransom expected for their release. Among the latter were many women and children, who were made to suffer cruel fatigue, hunger, and thirst, and artfully made to apprehend being carried to Jamaica, and sold as slaves, that they might the more earnestly endeavour to procure money for their ransom. When these poor creatures threw themselves on their knees, and, weeping and tearing their hair, begged of Morgan to let them return to their families, his brutal answer was, that "he came not there to listen to cries and lamentations, but to seek money." This idol of his soul, indeed, he sought from his comrades as well as his captives, and in such a manner that it is astonishing they did not blow his brains out.

Having accomplished their fatiguing march back to San Lorenzo, the buccaneers divided their spoil, and soon after separated with their vessels, most likely to go upon new expeditions. As for the arch-villain Morgan, he subsequently came to England, and received the honour of knighthood from the hands of Charles II., who afterwards sent him to Jamaica to fill a judicial office. Here he behaved with his wonted cruelty, and in a few years was transmitted home a prisoner at the instance of the Spanish court; but no charge being preferred against him, he was liberated. Circumstances such as these give us a curious insight into the state of morals towards the conclusion of the seventeenth century.

The plundering of Panama by Morgan fired the imaginations of the buccaneers, who now planned similarly daring expeditions to the South Sea, the coasts of which and their cities seemed to them like a newly discovered mine of wealth—a place where gold was to be had for the gathering. This became known to the Spaniards, and gave rise to numerous forebodings and prophecies, both in Spain and in Peru, of great invasions by land and sea.

After one or two ineffectual attempts of parties of pirates to cross the isthmus of Darien, an expedition was planned, in 1680, by a set of English adventurers, who found means to procure the friendship and co-operation of the Indians who inhabited the line of route. The buccaneers who engaged in this expedition were the crews of seven vessels, amounting altogether to 366 men, of whom thirty-seven were left to guard the ships during the absence of those who went on the expedition, which was not expected to be of long continuance. There were several men of some literary talent among the marauders, who have written accounts of the proceedings, which have the most romantic interest. These were Basil Ringrose, Barty Sharp, William Dampier, who, though a common seaman, was endowed with great observation and a talent for description, and Lionel Wafer, a surgeon providently engaged by the buccaneers.

It was on the 16th of April that the expedition passed over from Golden Island, and landed in Darien, each man provided with four cakes of bread, called dough-boys, with a fusil, a pistol, and a hanger. They began their arduous march marshalled in divisions, each with its commander and distinguishing flag. Many Darien Indians came to supply them with provisions, and to keep them company as confederates; among these were two chiefs, who went by the names of Captain Andreas and Captain Antonio.

After enduring tremendous fatigues, the party at length reached Santa Maria, a town situated on a river which falls into the South Sea. This place they plundered, and put to death numbers of the inhabitants. As their booty was not great, they resolved on pushing onwards by the river to the ocean. On the 17th of April the expedition embarked, and fell down the river to the gulf of San Miguel, which they did not reach until the following morning, owing to a flood-tide. They were now fairly in the South Sea! The prophecy of the Spaniards was accomplished, and the buccaneers looked across that magnificent expanse of waters with sanguine hope. On the 19th of April they entered the vast bay of Panama, and captured at one of the islands a Spanish vessel of thirty tons, on board of which one hundred and thirty of the buccaneers immediately threw themselves, overjoyed to be relieved from the cramped and crowded state they had endured in the canoes—though of a certainty, even now, so many men on board so small a vessel could leave small room for comfort.

It would be tiresome to recite minutely the adventures of these marauders. By means of their boats or canoes, they had the boldness to capture several vessels lying in the bay of Panama, and in less than a week from their appearance on the coast, they possessed a tolerably well equipped fleet. In the battles by which they had captured these ships, they lost a number of men; still this did not discourage them. They chose a new commander, one Richard Sawkins, in the room of their deceased leader, and prepared for a cruise. Panama was, luckily, now well fortified, and held out against their attacks. After staying ten days here to no purpose, they retired to the island of Taboga, in the neighbourhood. Here they stopped nearly a fortnight, in the expectation of the arrival of a rich ship from Lima. The ship came not, but several other vessels fell into their hands, by which they obtained nearly sixty thousand dollars in specie, twelve hundred sacks of flour, two thousand jars of wine, a quantity of brandy, sugar, sweetmeats, poultry, and other provisions, some gunpowder, shot, &c. Among their prisoners was a number of unfortunate negro slaves, which tempted the Spanish merchants of Panama to go to the buccaneers, and to buy as many of the slaves as they were inclined to sell. Those merchants paid two hundred pieces of eight for every negro, and they sold to the buccaneers all such stores and commodities as they stood in need of.

Ringrose, one of the buccaneers, relates, that during these communications the governor of Panama sent to demand of their leader, "Why, during a time of peace between England and Spain, Englishmen should come into those seas to commit injury?—and from whom they had their commission so to do?" Sawkins replied, "That he and his companions came to assist their friend, the king of Darien (the said chief Andreas), who was the rightful lord of Panama, and all the country thereabouts. That, as they had come so far, it was reasonable that they should receive some satisfaction for their trouble, and if the governor would send to them five hundred pieces of eight for each man, and one thousand for each commander, and would promise not any further to annoy the Darien Indians, their allies, that then the buccaneers would desist from hostilities, and go quietly about their business." The governor could scarcely be expected to comply with these moderate demands.

Tired of waiting for the rich ship from Lima, the buccaneers in a short time sailed on a cruise, determined to take whatever fell in their way. Generalising the account of their expeditions, it may be stated that they, from time to time, fell in with and captured both richly and poorly laden vessels; but quarrels among them about the division of the spoil were incessant, and they lost to one another by gambling their hard-won plunder. Diminished in numbers by their encounters to a crew of seventy men, under a new leader, Barty Sharp, they at length bethought themselves of returning to the Atlantic. While in this mind, they had the " good fortune," as they termed it, to pick up three valuable prizes. The first was a ship called the San Pedro, with a lading of cocoa-nuts, and 21,000 pieces of eight in chests, and 16,000 in bags, besides plate. The money in bags, with all the loose plunder, was immediately divided, each man receiving two hundred and thirty-four pieces of eight. The money in chests was reserved for a future division. Their second prize was a packet from Panama bound to Callao, by which they learned that in Panama it was believed that all the buccaneers had returned over land to the West Indies. The third was a ship called the San Rosario, which made a bold resistance, and did not submit until her captain was killed. She came from Callao with a cargo of wine, brandy, oil, and fruit, and had in her as much money as yielded ninety-four dollars to each buccaneer. Through their ignorance of metals, they missed a much greater booty. There were seven hundred pigs of plate which they mistook for tin, on account of its not being refined and fitted for coining. They only took one of the seven hundred pigs, and two-thirds of this they melted down into bullets, and otherwise squandered away. After having beaten along the coast, coming at times to anchor, making a few discoveries, and giving names to islands and bays, but taking no prizes, they sailed early in November from the shores of Patagonia. Their navigation hence was more than could be imagined; it was like the journey of travellers by night in a strange country without a guide. The weather being very stormy, they were afraid to venture through the strait of Magellan, but ran to the south to go round Terra del Fuego. Spite of tempests, clouds, and darkness, and immense icebergs, they doubled in safety the redoubtable Cape Horn, after a cruise of nearly twelve months' duration.

These ocean robbers had the fortune to be left in quiet possession of their spoils. Two or three were tried and hanged, but on this, as on other occasions, the bulk of the party were never called to account, or if they were, they found means by bribes to escape a well-deserved punishment. Some had even the impudence to write and publish narratives of their piratical expeditions; and a sort of apology for their crimes has been hazarded in modern times, on account of their discoveries in the South Seas.

One of the last of the class of sea robbers we have been noticing, was the noted Captain Kid, who figured principally as a rover in the East Indian seas. This worthy finished his career on the gallows at Execution Dock in London, in the year 1701. His memory has been preserved in a doggrel ballad, beginning, if we recollect properly, with the lines—

> "My name was Captain Kid,
> When I sail'd, when I sail'd,
> My name was Captain Kid,
> When I sailed.
>
> I roamed from sound to sound,
> And many a ship I found,
> And them I sank or burn'd,
> When I sail'd, when I sail'd."

The foregoing sketch is presented with the view of giving our readers an idea of the lawless state of society at a period as late as the close of the seventeenth century, and, therefore, of showing by contrast the improvement which has since taken place in national manners. Fortunately for commerce, and the friendly intercourse betwixt nations, all systematic piracy on a great scale, such as we have alluded to, has been long since extirpated by the concurring efforts of every civilised power.

ALEXANDER SELKIRK.

This extraordinary man, whose solitary residence on the island of Juan Fernandez suggested to De Foe the matchless fiction of Robinson Crusoe, was a native of Largo, a village on the north shore of the Firth of Forth, in Scotland. He was the son of a thriving country shoemaker, named John Selkirk or Selcraig, and was born in the year 1676. Though he displayed some aptitude at school, especially in learning navigation, he was a restless and troublesome youth, of a quarrelsome temper, and almost always engaged in mischief. His father was one of those stern disciplinarians who formerly abounded in Scotland, and whose severity in dictating repulsive exercises and restraining from innocent indulgences, was so frequently rewarded, in the case of children of lively temperaments, with effects so different from what were expected. The mother, on the other hand, who was soft and pliant, made the subject of our memoir a favourite, on account of his being a seventh son, born without the intervention of a daughter; which in her opinion marked him out for a lucky destiny. The boy's own wish was to go to sea; that of his father, to keep him at home as an assistant in his own trade; and it appears that the mother advocated the views of her son, as most likely to lead to the realisation of her superstitious hopes. It must be allowed that these circumstances, operating in a humble walk of life, at the time and place alluded to, were not calculated to soothe an irritable, control a reckless, or even to preserve the original features of an amiable character.

After working till about his twentieth year at his father's trade, Alexander Selkirk left his native village, in order to avoid ecclesiastical censure for domestic quarrelling, and was at sea for four years. On his return in 1701, he once more excited public scandal by his conduct in the family circle; and being again cited by the kirk-session, along with his father, mother, and other relations, he on this occasion gave satisfaction, by submitting to a rebuke in church, and promising amendment. Having spent the winter at home, he returned in spring to England, in search of employment as a mariner. The war of the Spanish succession was now breaking out, and among the means adopted by Britain for distressing the enemy, was the employment of those daring half piratical commodores, who used to scour the South Seas at all seasons in search of Spanish merchantmen and bullion-ships, allowing no regular principle of warfare, except that there never was peace beyond the Line. The celebrated Captain Dampier had projected an enterprise with two well-armed vessels, under the commission of the admiralty; designing to sail up the river La Plata, and seize a few of the rich galleons which usually sailed once a-year from that port to the mother country. His vessels were respectively entitled the St George and the Cinque Ports, of twenty-six and sixteen guns; and Selkirk, who was probably recommended by experience in the same kind of employment, was appointed sailing-master of the smaller ship. The terms on which both officers and men entered this expedition were very simple: they were to have no wages beyond a certain share of their prizes. Such, however, had been the success of many previous expeditions of the same kind, that no doubt was entertained by any one on board, that they would each return with an immense load of Spanish gold. The two vessels sailed in September 1703, but were too late for the galleons, all of which had got into port before they reached Madeira. Dampier then relinquished his design upon the river La Plata, and resolved to attack some rich town on the Spanish main. But before they left this range of isles, dissensions began to break out, and, by orders of Dampier, the first lieutenant of the St George, with whom he had quarrelled, was left with his servant upon

St Jago. They soon after reached the coast of Brazil, where they had the misfortune to lose Captain Pickering of the Cinque Ports, who was acknowledged to be the most sensible man on board, and the main stay of the enterprise. This vessel was now very leaky, and falling under the command of a man of brutal character named Stradling, it was no longer a place of comfort for Selkirk, who about this time had a dream, which he esteemed as a forewarning of the failure of the expedition and the loss of the Cinque Ports, and formed the resolution to withdraw at the first opportunity. The situation of the men in general may be guessed from the fact, that nine of the crew of the St George went ashore upon the isle of La Granda, preferring the hazard of perpetual slavery among the Spaniards, to continuing any longer with their countrymen. The two vessels now doubled Cape Horn, and sailed for the isle of Juan Fernandez, where they were refitted. Here, however, a violent quarrel broke out between Stradling and his crew, forty-two of whom (probably including Selkirk) went ashore, vowing that they would not return to the vessel, in which there were not now so many as twenty men left. It was not without great difficulty, nor till they had become somewhat tired of the island, that they could be prevailed upon to change their resolution. For some months after this revolt, the two vessels cruised along the coast of Chili, capturing a few worthless merchant vessels, which supplied them with fresh stores, but altogether failing in the principal object of their expedition. At length, Dampier and Stradling parted company, and the Cinque Ports returned to Juan Fernandez to refit.

Stradling and Selkirk had for some time been on such terms, that the latter was now determined to remain upon the island, the capability of which to support him was proved by two men, who had lived upon it since the vessels were there in spring. Accordingly, when the vessel was about to weigh, he went into a boat with all his effects, and was rowed ashore under the direction of the captain (October 1704). His first sensation on landing was one of joy, arising from the novelty of an exemption from the annoyances which had been oppressing him for such a length of time; but he no sooner heard the strokes of the receding oars, than the sense of solitude and helplessness fell upon his mind, and made him rush into the water to entreat his companions to take him once more on board. The brutal commander only made this change of resolution a subject of mockery, and told him it would be best for the remainder of the crew that so troublesome a fellow should remain where he was.

Here, then, was a single human being left to provide for his own subsistence upon an uninhabited and uncultivated isle, far from all the haunts of his kind,* and with but slender hopes of ever again mingling with his fellow creatures. Vigorous as the mind of Selkirk appears to have been, it sank for some days under the horrors of his situation, and he could do nothing but sit upon his chest, and gaze in the direction in which the ship had vanished, vainly hoping for its return. On partly recovering his equanimity, he found it necessary to consider the means of continuing existence. The stores which he had brought ashore, consisted, besides his clothing and bedding, of a firelock, a pound of gunpowder, a quantity of bullets, a flint and steel, a few pounds of tobacco, a hatchet, a knife, a kettle, a flip-can, a bible, some books of devotion, and one or two concerning navigation, and his mathematical instruments. The island he knew to contain wild goats; but being unwilling to lose the chance of observing a passing sail,

* Juan Fernandez, so called from a Spanish pilot who discovered it in 1572, is 330 miles from the nearest land in South America. It is situated in latitude 33 degrees 40 minutes south, and in longitude 78 degrees 52 minutes west. It was several times occupied, both before and after Selkirk's time, by families prosecuting trade, and even by solitary mariners, left by chance or otherwise. In 1823, Lord Cochrane found it destitute of inhabitants; but, according to very recent information, it now supports about 400 people, who acknowledge the Chilian government, and are ruled over by an Englishman named Sutcliffe.

he preferred for a long time feeding upon shell-fish and seals, which he found upon the shore. The island, which is rugged and picturesque, but covered by luxuriant vegetation, and clothed to the tops of the hills with wood, was now in all the bloom and freshness of spring; but upon the dejected solitary, its charms were spent in vain. He could only wander along the beach, pining for the approach of some friendly vessel, which might restore him, under however unpleasant circumstances, to the converse of his fellow creatures.

At length the necessity of providing a shelter from the weather, supplied him with an occupation that served in some measure to divert his thoughts. He built himself two huts with the wood of the pimento tree, thatching them with the long grass which grows upon the island. One was to serve him as a kitchen, the other as a bedroom. But yet, every day for the first eighteen months, he spent more or less time on the beach, watching for the appearance of a sail upon the horizon. At the end of that time, partly through habit, partly through the influence of religion, which here awakened in full force upon his mind, he became reconciled to his situation. Every morning after rising, he read a portion of Scripture, sang a psalm, and prayed, speaking aloud in order to preserve the use of his voice; he afterwards remarked, that, during his residence on the island, he was a better Christian than he had ever been before, or would probably ever be again. He at first lived much upon turtles, which abounded upon the shores, but afterwards found himself able to run down the wild goats, whose flesh he either roasted or stewed, and of which he kept a small stock, tamed, around his dwelling, to be used in the event of his being disabled by sickness. One of the greatest inconveniences which afflicted him for the first few months, was the want of salt; but he gradually became accustomed to this privation, and at last found so much relish in unsalted food, that, after being restored to society, it was with equal difficulty that he reconciled himself to take it in any other condition. As a substitute for bread he had turnips, parsnips, and the cabbage palm, all of excellent quality, and also radishes and water-cresses. When his clothes were worn out, he supplied their place with goat-skins, which gave him an appearance much more uncouth than any wild animal. He had a piece of linen, from which he made new shirts by means of a nail and the thread of his stockings; and he never wanted this comfortable piece of attire during the whole period of his residence on the island. Every physical want being thus gratified, and his mind soothed by devotional feeling, he at length began to positively enjoy his existence, often lying for whole days in the delicious bowers which he had formed for himself, abandoned to the most pleasant sensations.

Among the quadruped inhabitants of the isle were multitudes of rats, which at the first annoyed him by gnawing his feet while asleep. Against this enemy he found it necessary to enter into a treaty, offensive and defensive, with the cats, which also abounded in his neighbourhood. Having caught and tamed some of the latter animals, he was soon freed from the presence of the rats, but not without some disagreeable consequences, in the reflection, that, should he die in his hut, his friendly auxiliaries would probably be obliged, for their subsistence, to devour his body. He was in the meantime able to turn them to some account for his amusement, by teaching them to dance and perform a number of antic feats, such as cats are not in general supposed capable of learning, but which they might probably acquire, if any individual in civilised life were able to take the necessary pains. Another of his amusements was hunting on foot, in which he at length, through healthy exercise and habit, became such a proficient, that he could run down the swiftest goat. Some of the young of these animals he taught to dance in company with his kittens; and he often afterwards declared, that he never danced with a lighter heart or greater spirit than to the sound of his own voice in the midst of these dumb companions.

Selkirk was careful during his stay on the island to

measure the lapse of time, and distinguish Sunday from the other days of the week. Anxious, in the midst of all his indifference to society, that, in the event of his dying in solitude, his having lived there might not be unknown to his fellow-creatures, he carved his name upon a number of trees, adding the date of his being left, and the period of time which had since elapsed. When his knife was worn out, he made new ones, and even a cleaver for his meat, out of some hoops which he found on the shore. He several times saw vessels passing the island, but only two cast anchor beside it. Afraid of being taken by the Spaniards, who would have consigned him to hopeless captivity, he endeavoured to ascertain whether these strangers were so or not, before making himself known. In both cases he found them enemies; and on one of the occasions, having approached too near, he was observed and chased, and only escaped by taking refuge in a tree. At length, on the last day of January 1709, four years and four months from the commencement of his solitary life, he had the unspeakable satisfaction of observing two British vessels approach, evidently with the intention of touching at the island. The night having fallen before they came near, he kindled a large fire on the beach, to inform the strangers that a human being was there. During the night, hope having banished all desire of sleep, he employed himself in killing goats, and preparing a feast of fresh meat for those whom he expected to be his deliverers. In the morning he found that the vessels had removed to a greater distance, but, ere long, a boat left the side of one of them, and approached the shore. Selkirk ran joyfully to meet his countrymen, waving a linen rag to attract their attention; and having pointed out to them a proper landing-place, soon had the satisfaction of clasping them in his arms. Joy at first deprived him of that imperfect power of utterance which solitude had left to him, and the strangers were for a time so surprised by his rude habiliments, long beard, and savage appearance, as to be in much the same condition. But in a little they were mutually able to make explanations, when it appeared that the two vessels, called the Duke and Duchess, formed a privateering expedition similar to that of Dampier, but under the command of Captain Woodes Rogers, the former commander being here employed only as pilot. Dover, the second captain, and Fry, the lieutenant, of Rogers's own vessel, were of the boat party, and after partaking of Selkirk's hospitality, invited him on board. But so little eager was he to leave his solitude, that he was not prevailed upon to do so, till assured that Dampier had no situation of command in the expedition. He was then brought on board the Duke, along with his principal effects, and, by the recommendation of Dampier, who said he had been the best man in the Cinque Ports, was engaged as a mate. He now found that if he had remained on board the Cinque Ports, he must have experienced a worse fate than his late solitude, for, soon after leaving Juan Fernandez, Stradling had been obliged to surrender himself and his crew to the Spaniards, on account of the leaky state of the vessel, and had ever since been in confinement.

A few weeks after leaving the island, Selkirk was appointed to the command of a prize which was fitted out as a privateer, and in this situation he conducted himself with a degree of vigour and prudence that reflects credit on his character. The business in which he was engaged was certainly one by no means calculated to give play to the more amiable qualities of human nature; but even in the sacking of coast towns, and expeditions of plunder into the interior, which for months formed his chief employment, our hero seems to have mingled humanity in as high a proportion as possible with the execution of his duty. The expedition of Rogers was as remarkable for steadiness, resolution, and success, as that of Dampier had been for quarrelling and indecision; and it excites a curious feeling of surprise when we learn that the church of England service was regularly read on the quarter-decks of these piratical vessels, and all hands piped to prayers before every action. Selkirk proved himself, by his steadiness, decent manners, and religious turn of mind, a most appropriate member of the corps commanded by Rogers, and was accordingly much valued by his superiors. At the beginning of the ensuing year, the vessels began their voyage across the Pacific, with the design of returning by the East Indies, and in this part of the enterprise Selkirk acted as sailing-master. They did not, however, reach England till October 1711, when Selkirk had been absent from his country for eight years. Of the enormous sum of £170,000 which Rogers had realised by plundering the enemy, Selkirk seems to have shared to the amount of about £800.

His singular history was soon made known to the public, and, immediately after his arrival in London, he became an object of curiosity, not only to the people at large, but to those elevated by rank and learning. Sir Richard Steele, some time after, devoted to him an article in the paper entitled The Englishman, in which he tells the reader, that, as Selkirk is a man of good sense, it is a matter of great curiosity to hear him give an account of the different revolutions of his mind during the term of his solitude. " When I first saw him," continues this writer, " I thought, if I had not been let into his character and story, I could have discovered that he had been much separated from company, *from his aspect and gesture;* there was a strong but cheerful seriousness in his look, and a certain disregard of the ordinary things about him, as if he had been sunk in thought. When the ship which brought him off the island came in, he received them with the greatest indifference with relation to the prospect of going off with them, but with great satisfaction in an opportunity to refresh and help them. The man frequently bewailed his return to the world, which could not, he said, with all its enjoyments, restore him to the tranquillity of his solitude. Though I had frequently conversed with him, after a few months' absence he met me in the street, and though he spoke to me, I could not recollect that I had seen him: *familiar converse in this*

F

town had taken off the loneliness of his aspect, and quite altered the air of his face." What makes this latter circumstance the more remarkable, is the fact of nearly three years having elapsed between his restoration to society and the time when Sir Richard Steele first saw him.

In the spring of 1712, Selkirk returned on a Sunday forenoon to his native village, and finding that his friends were at church, went thither, and for some time sat eyeing them without being recognised, a suit of elegant gold-laced clothes perhaps helping to preserve his incognito. At length his mother, after gazing on him for some time, uttered a cry of joy, and flew to his arms. For some days he felt pleasure in the society of his friends, but in time began to pine for other scenes, his mind still reverting with regret to his lost solitude. It would appear, indeed, that so long an absence from society had in some measure unfitted him for it. He tried solitary fishing, built a bower like that of Juan Fernandez in the garden behind his brother's house, and wandered for days in the picturesque solitude of a glen beneath the brow of Largo Law. But nothing could compensate for the meditative life which he had lost. At length, having formed an attachment to a rustic maiden, named Sophia Bruce, whom he met in the glen just named, he suddenly disappeared with her, and never more was seen at Largo. In 1717 he once more went to sea. Nothing else is known respecting him, except that he died in the situation of lieutenant on board the ship Weymouth, in the year 1723, leaving a widow, who afterwards realised his patrimony at Largo, consisting of one small house.

The house in which he lived during his last residence at Largo, is still occupied by the descendants of his brother, who preserve his chest and cup. His flip-can exists in the possession of another relation, who once did the present writer the favour of showing it to him; and his gun has for some years been the property of Major Lumsden of Lathallan, near Largo.

PERILS OF A DUTCH CREW WINTERING AT NOVA ZEMBLA.

TOWARDS the close of the sixteenth century, the spirit for commercial adventure made rapid progress in Holland, and various companies were formed to promote the interests of traffic. Sensible of the great advantages that would result from shortening the voyage from Europe to the distant climates of the East, the Dutch were at an early period occupied in searching for a passage by the north, which, according to the geographical opinions prevailing in that age, would conduct their fleets to China, Japan, and other places, in half the usual time. Though their attempts in this respect ultimately proved abortive, they were not void of utility, and led to some interesting incidents, which are partly contained in the following narrative:—

Three ships sailed from the Texel in 1594, accompanied by a fishing-bark, for the purpose of discovering the northern passage, and reached as far as 77° 45' of north latitude, when a vast surface of ice, extending to the utmost limits of the horizon, obstructed their progress. Their commanders, after betaking themselves to the boats, and examining those creeks and shores which they were able to gain, considered it impracticable to proceed, and returned to Holland in about fourteen weeks from their departure.

Notwithstanding this disappointment, another voyage was resolved upon, and its success so confidently anticipated, that no less than seven vessels, six of which were laden with commodities for eastern traffic, sailed on the same pursuit, in the course of the following year. These vessels found Russians collecting whale oil and the teeth of the sea-cow in latitude 72° or 73° north, with whom they interchanged mutual civilities, and saw a race of people, whom they called Samoides, at the entrance of the Waygat's Straits. Soon afterwards, the ice opposed their advancing towards the north-east, into what they supposed the open ocean;

thick fogs prevailed, and a continual change of wind. They passed through the Waygat's Straits, however, and landed at Statten Island; thence surveying the surrounding sea, and observing great quantities of ice drifting from the east, they returned through the Straits, and abandoned the passage as impracticable.

Though these successive failures repressed the ardour of the Dutch, they did not lose sight of an object which they had viewed with such predilection; and two vessels were once more fitted out at the charge of the city of Amsterdam, for resuming the voyage of discovery by the north. One of them was commanded by Jacob Hemskirk, an experienced mariner, with whom was conjoined William Barentz, as pilot, a navigator enjoying equal reputation, and who had, besides, been out in both the preceding voyages. In the same vessel also, was Gerard de Veer, the author of the only history of all the calamities and adventures which ensued in prosecution of the enterprise. John Cornelius Ryp was master or supercargo of the other.

On the 22d of May 1596, the two ships left Holland, and soon afterwards a strange phenomenon was observed in the heavens, consisting of three suns, all visible at a time, each within a parhelion, and a rainbow traversing the whole : besides which, other two rainbows likewise appeared.

Detached flakes of ice were seen floating on the 5th of June, which the people on board at first sight took for a flock of swans swimming in the sea, until a nearer approach proved their error. Sailing through water of a deep green colour, they discovered an island about five miles long, in 74° 30' north latitude, on which they landed.

The party with Barentz having descried a white bear in the sea, pursued it in the boat, in hopes of being able to cast a noose round its neck. But on closing with the animal, its size and menacing aspect deterred them, until they obtained a reinforcement of men and arms. Yet during four glasses that a renewed encounter lasted with the bear, all their exertions to destroy it proved unavailing; and it actually swam away with an axe struck into its back. The boat followed, and one of the men at length cleft its head asunder by the blow of a hatchet. The skin of this enormous animal was twelve feet long, but the people did not relish the flesh. The incident induced them to name the land " Bear's Island."

Prosecuting their voyage, they got so far north as 80° 11', where after a combat almost equally severe, another bear, whose skin was thirteen feet long, was killed; and they found vast numbers of wild geese hatching their eggs on land in that high latitude. Ranging along the coast, they found a good haven, but could get no farther north on account of fields of ice. The navigation was therefore pursued in somewhat lower latitudes, wherever the ice gave access, until the 1st of July, when Barentz and John Cornelius Ryp, disagreeing about the course to be followed, parted while in sight of Bear's Island.

On the 17th of July, Barentz saw the coast of Nova Zembla, near Lom's Bay, and three days afterwards, being obstructed by the ice, anchored at Cross Isle. Here eight men, having gone ashore unarmed, had a narrow escape from the pursuit of two bears.

The vessel was now amidst extensive fields of ice, and huge masses, to which she was occasionally secured in her progress, appeared floating, or had run aground. One of these was calculated to be sixteen fathoms above the water, and thirty-six under it, that is, more than three hundred feet from the summit to the base. The great fields of ice began to break up, with a noise like thunder, on the 10th of August, and the ship being fast to a huge piece aground, not less than four hundred, of smaller size, were driven past her by a current. Lest she should be carried away by the ice, she was brought nearer the coast, into a more sheltered station; but it was soon necessary to shift her anchorage, according as circumstances required.

Climbing to the top of a lofty mountain in Nova Zembla, the mariners were encouraged with the prospect of an open sea towards the south-east, and concluded that they should thence be able to accomplish the voyage. But after repeated difficulties, losing a boat and also the ship's rudder, they were completely surrounded by ice on the 27th of August. Temporary intervals, wherein the ice separated, succeeded; but at last the ship was enclosed and frozen in on all sides, so that the people were obliged to have recourse to the shore.

There they found a fresh-water river about two miles inland, and saw the traces of animals, which they conceived to be deer: great store of wood likewise lay near the river, consisting of entire trees with the roots, drifted from other countries. Thus having no alternative, the Dutch resolved to winter in this desolate region.

Meantime, the ice accumulated greatly round the vessel: her prow was raised far above its surface, while the stern, sunk behind, was crushed together in such a manner, that the cracking of the timbers rendered the mariners apprehensive she would be utterly destroyed. They had dragged their boat over the ice to the land, and in the next place got out a quantity of arms, ammunition, and provisions, wherewithal to fortify themselves against wild beasts and hunger during their dreary abode.

On the 14th of September, they began to collect the drift wood for building a hut, and prepared sledges, with which it was with great labour drawn over the ice and snow, near to the place where the vessel lay. Thirteen men were employed in dragging the sledges, and three in preparing each ladening of wood; but they could make no more than two trips a-day, from fatigue and the approaching darkness.

Whilst thus industriously occupied, the carpenter unfortunately died on the 23d of September, and was next day interred by his surviving comrades in the cleft of a hill, as the ground was too hard for them to dig a grave. There were now sixteen persons in all, but some of the number were frequently indisposed.

The rafters of the hut were laid, though, on account

of excessive cold, the people were scarce able to work; and if any of them chanced to put a nail in his mouth, as workmen are wont to do, it stuck to the skin, and blood followed its removal. Nothing but urgent necessity could have induced them to continue their operations. A great fire was kindled all around the hut, to thaw the earth, that they might bring it up, and make the under part a little closer: the ground, however, was frozen so very hard and deep, that it would not yield on that occasion, and there would have been too great a waste of wood in trying it again.

The people having shot a bear, took out its entrails, and set it upright on its four legs to freeze, in which state they meant, if possible, to carry it to Holland. Some time afterwards, a seaman being suddenly surprised and pursued by another bear, hastily ran towards the ship, with the bear following him, until it reached the first, now frozen over, and totally covered, except one of the paws: here the animal made a stop, and allowed the man time to save his life.

At length the hut was finished on the 12th of October 1595, when half the crew left the ship, to sleep that night ashore: but they suffered severely from the cold, owing to scarcity of bed-clothes; and as the chimney was not completed, the smoke in the hut was intolerable.

In the next place, the launch was dragged ashore with incredible difficulty; and as the absence of the sun was about to leave the seamen in perpetual night, they made all possible haste to land the remainder of the provisions required. They had no hopes of the vessel floating, on which account the rudder was also carried away for preservation, until the ice might thaw in the succeeding year.

The preparations for wintering in Nova Zembla were completed while the sun was still visible from the surface of the earth. On the 30th of October, a lamp was fitted to burn all night, and supplied with melted fat of bears which had been killed for oil. On the 2d of November, only part of the sun was seen in the horizon; and on the 4th he had sunk entirely under it.

At this time the surgeon contrived a bath for the people in a cask, which was found extremely salutary and beneficial, from their confinement. Setting traps in the neighbourhood, they caught white foxes, which began to be quite common, whereas the bears had entirely left them as the sun disappeared; and their flesh, resembling that of a rabbit, was much relished by the people. A device was soon adopted of placing the traps, so that the captured animal could immediately be drawn into the hut.

On distributing the bread, each man's allowance was restricted to four pounds five ounces in eight days; and as the strength of the beer brought ashore had been destroyed by successive freezing and thawing, each had two small cups of wine daily. A large Dutch cheese was ate by the whole company, and sixteen remaining delivered to the people, each being left to his own economy.

Repeated storms of snow, at this period, began to block up the hut without; and within, the cold was almost insupportable. While the people washed their linen, it froze immediately when taken out of warm water: nay, one side froze while the other was next the fire. They were almost suffocated from the closeness of the hut not allowing proper vent to the smoke; but the fire falling rather lower than usual for some days, ice formed two inches thick on the floor, and the beds were even covered with it. Except when cooking their provisions, the people lay constantly in bed, and then they heard such explosions among the ice at sea, as could only be occasioned by huge mountains bursting asunder, and tumbling down into a confused heap of fragments. Intense cold having stopped their clock, though additional weights were hung to it, they prepared a twelve-hour sand-glass, to enable them to ascertain how the time passed.

The cold was so intense on the 6th of December, that they scarce expected to be able to survive it. Nothing could keep them in heat: their wine froze, and they were obliged to melt it every two days, when half a pint was served out to each man. It was their only liquid except snow water; a beverage not very suitable to their condition.

Before this time, the day was so dark, that the mariners could not distinguish it from night: so that on one occasion, when perplexed by the stopping of the clock, they continued in bed, believing it was still night; and on another occasion they only knew that it was night by the moon shining bright, and remaining constantly above the horizon.

On the 7th of December, they considered it necessary to repair to the vessel for some coal that had been left in her, and with this made a good fire in the evening, which revived them greatly. To enjoy its comfort as much as possible, they sat up late, and closed all the apertures of their hut to keep in the heat. But a seaman, already indisposed, who could bear the effect of the fire less than the others, began to complain, and all soon found themselves attacked with giddiness; whence they could scarce stand until opening the door. In fact, he who first reached it, swooning away, fell out on the snow. Gerard de Veer, however, recovered him by sprinkling vinegar in his face, and the admission of the fresh air removed the sensations overcoming the others. The captain then distributed a glass of wine to the men to strengthen them.

The leather of the seamen's shoes was now frozen to such a degree of hardness, that they could not use them; on which account they made a kind of slippers of skins, and put several pairs of socks over one another to increase the heat. The ice stood an inch thick on the sides of the hut, and when they went out in clear weather, their clothes were whitened with frost and shining icicles. The fire was increased within, taking the precaution of leaving the chimney open, that the smoke might get vent.

Many stars being visible on a clear night, the Dutch, by an observation on the 14th of January 1597, found themselves in 76° of north latitude. About that time the wood brought into the hut being all consumed, they began to shovel away the snow on the outside, to come at more, which, on account of the excessive rigour of the weather, was with difficulty accomplished.

Seven of their number next repaired to the ship, and found the ice had risen higher within, and that she was still fast frozen up. In the cabin they caught a fox, which was carried home and eaten.

Several successive days of stormy weather confined the mariners to their hut. There they heard the foxes running over it, and, as their provisions were beginning to decline, regretted that they could not catch them. But the intense cold almost absorbed all other sensations, and they had recourse to hot stones laid on their feet and bodies, to keep them warm. However, they comforted themselves, that, as the sun was now at the lowest, he would not be long of returning to gladden them with his view. While sitting before the fire, their backs would be quite white with the frost, and, on stretching their feet towards it for warmth, their stockings would be burnt before they began to feel its influence. A cloth hoisted on a pole, thrust up through the chimney, to show the direction of the wind, immediately became stiff and inflexible.

In this way did the year 1596 terminate, and 1597 begin.

Though it proved necessary to diminish the allowance of wine, when twelfth night arrived the seamen requested the captain to permit them all to make merry, with some savings of the wine, which several, instead of consuming, had stored up. Therefore, they made pancakes with meal and oil, and, soaking biscuit among wine, were as jovial as if they had been at home in their own houses in Holland.

Again visiting the ship, it was evident to them that bears of different sizes had been there, and on striking a light, and going below, they found the ice a foot higher than formerly. Almost despairing that the vessel would ever float again, they thought it prudent to spare the remaining coals, lest they might find themselves obliged to attempt navigating homewards in the open launch.

The foxes, in the next place, beginning to disappear, indicated the return of bears; for so long as the latter retreated, the former came out, and were but little seen when the bears were numerous.

On the 24th of January, the day being clear, with a west wind, Gerard de Veer, Jacob Hemskirk, and another, went down to the sea-side, towards the south of Nova Zembla, from whence they unexpectedly saw the edge of the sun above the horizon. They hastened to impart the welcome tidings to Barentz and their other companions; but their report was discredited; for Barentz affirmed that it was too early for his return by fourteen days. The two following days being dark and cloudy, doubts of the fact were still further entertained, and many of the people positively affirmed that it was impossible. On the 26th, a man died who had been some time sick, and next morning his comrades, with great difficulty, owing to the excessive cold, dug a grave for him in the snow, seven feet deep. Having performed the last offices to him, attended by such funeral service as circumstances would admit, they returned within the hut to breakfast. Then discoursing concerning the prodigious quantity of snow which unremittingly fell in the place, they said among themselves, that, if again blocked up by it, they should find a way of climbing out through the chimney; accordingly, the captain tried the experiment, while another going out of the hut to ascertain whether he succeeded, saw the complete orb of the sun above the horizon.

The weather still remained uncertain, though the people, relieved from the tedium of perpetual night, took exercise to strengthen them. But their hut was repeatedly blocked up by snow; and to avoid the labour of always clearing it away from the door, they on those occasions found an exit by the chimney.

Bears began to return along with the sun, and one which was killed afforded at least a hundred pounds of grease, which the seamen melted for their lamp. But a number of foxes coming to devour the carcase, the apprehension of other bears being attracted hither induced them to bury it deep under the snow. They considered it expedient to collect more wood for fuel, dragging it on a sledge as before ; however, their strength being much reduced, their task was accomplished with far greater labour. Though the cold moderated for a time towards the end of February, its rigour increased about the middle of March, and on the 24th of that month the hut was totally blocked up.

At last the sea began to open, though the mariners despaired of disengaging the ship, or of rendering her serviceable for a voyage. Still she was hemmed in by ice, sometimes heaped in mountains around her: and their anxiety was increased by observing that, about the middle of March, the sea was so open that the vessel was within seventy-five paces of it; whereas, a new frost increased the distance on the 4th of May to five hundred paces.

Thus the only means of quitting Nova Zembla seemed to consist in the launch and boat; but the 29th of May arrived before the people attempted to dig either out of the snow. However willing, their reduced strength rendered their progress slow; and after they had laboured hard, compelled them to desist: on another trial they were put to flight by a bear. Six days' work at length enabled them to put the launch in a condition to be dragged over the hard ice and snow to the ship. There they sawed off the stern, which was narrow, and built one broader and higher, so that it might be better adapted to stand the sea.

The boat was in the same way got out of the snow, and dragged to the ship, as also several sledges laden with articles from the hut. These operations occupied a long time; they were frequently interrupted, and ultimately accomplished with great difficulty, from the state of the weather and repeated dangers. Nevertheless, on the 12th of June nothing remained but to smooth the way for the launch and boat, down to the water's edge, and drag them along on the 13th.

This being done, William Barentz, the pilot, wrote a brief recital of what had happened: that he and his companions had left Holland for the purpose of sailing to China by the north; but their ship being frozen up by ice, they were compelled, amidst many hardships, to winter ashore. The narrative he put into a musket barrel, hung up in the chimney of the hut, lest any mariners in future might experience a like adventure. The captain also thought it proper to obtain the subscription of his company to a narrative of their dangers and distresses, and of the necessity to which they were at last reduced, of hazarding a voyage homewards in two open boats.

Eleven loads of goods were in the next place dragged to the water's edge, and then William Barentz and Claes Andrisz, who had long been sick, were drawn on a sledge from the hut to the boats. The whole company was equally divided, and one of the sick attached to each, and on the 14th of June 1597, after ten months' dreary residence, the mariners set sail with a westerly wind from Nova Zembla.

After undergoing innumerable hardships, the twelve surviving mariners reached Holland, and, to the admiration of the citizens of Amsterdam, appeared in their Nova Zembla apparel. The fame of their adventures was soon disseminated, and they were carried from thence, to entertain the foreign ambassadors at the Hague with a recital of what had befallen them.

ESCAPE FROM A SHARK.

HARDY, in his Travels through Mexico, gives the following lively account of an escape from a shark:—
" The Placer de la Piedra Negada, which is near Loretta, was supposed to have quantities of very large pearl-oysters around it—a supposition which was at once confirmed by the great difficulty of finding this sunken rock. Don Pablo, however, succeeded in sounding it, and, in search of specimens of the largest and oldest shells, dived down in eleven fathoms water. The rock is not above 150 or 200 yards in circumference,

and our adventurer swam round and examined it in all directions, but without meeting any inducement to prolong his stay. Accordingly, being satisfied that there were no oysters, he thought of ascending to the surface of the water; but first he cast a look upwards, as all divers are obliged to do, who hope to avoid the hungry jaws of a monster. If the coast is clear, they may then rise without apprehension. Don Pablo, however, when he cast a hasty glance upwards, found that a tintetero had taken a station about three or four yards immediately above him, and, most probably, had been watching during the whole time that he had been down. A double-pointed stick is a useless weapon against a tintetero, as its mouth is of such enormous dimensions, that both man and stick would be swallowed together. He therefore felt himself rather nervous, as his retreat was now completely intercepted. But, under water, time is too precious to be spent in reflection, and therefore he swam round to another part of the rock, hoping by this artifice to avoid the vigilance of his persecutor. What was his dismay when he again looked up to find the pertinacious tintetero still hovering over him, as a hawk would follow a bird! He described him as having large, round, and inflamed eyes, apparently just ready to dart from their sockets with eagerness, and a mouth (at the recollection of which he still shuddered) that was constantly opening and shutting, as if the monster was already in imagination devouring his victim, or, at least, that the contemplation of his prey imparted a foretaste of the *goût!* Two alternatives now presented themselves to the mind of Don Pablo; one, to suffer himself to be drowned; the other, to be eaten. He had already been under water so considerable a time, that he found it impossible any longer to retain his breath, and was on the point of giving himself up for lost, with as much philosophy as he possessed. But what is dearer than life? The invention of man is seldom at a loss to find expedients for its preservation in cases of great extremity. On a sudden he recollected that on one side of the rock he had observed a sandy spot, and to this he swam with all imaginable speed; his attentive friend still watching his movements, and keeping a measured pace with him. As soon as he reached the spot, he commenced stirring it with his pointed stick, in such a way that the fine particles rose, and rendered the water perfectly turbid, so that he could not see the monster, nor the monster him. Availing himself of the *cloud* by which himself and the tintetero were enveloped, he swam very far out in a transvertical direction, and reached the surface in safety, although completely exhausted. Fortunately, he rose close to one of the boats; and those who were within, seeing him in such a state, and knowing that an enemy must have been persecuting him, and that by some artifice he had saved his life, jumped overboard, as is their common practice in such cases, to frighten the creature away by splashing in the water; and Don Pablo was taken into the boat more dead than alive."

CROSSING THE LINE.

THE following account of the ceremonies customary among sailors in crossing the equator, is the composition of a gentleman who has actually witnessed, and borne a part (that of a sufferer) in them.

I sailed from Portsmouth in April 1814, in an East India vessel of a thousand tons. There were seventeen passengers besides myself, the only youth amongst them. The most conspicuous of the number was an old corpulent general, who regularly took his two bottles of port every day after dinner, and then strutted upon deck with an extremely comical oscillation of gait. He was accompanied by his wife, a pretty lively creature of seventeen, happy in her recent emancipation from boarding-school control. Jokes innumerable were shot off at the old gentleman, who, with a fat good nature, was always the first to laugh at them himself. Even when these were practical, they did not put him out of humour:—for instance, a waggish officer observing that in his after-dinner walks he was in the habit, when the weather was warm, of leaving his hat on the capstan, took it up slily, and covered the lining with tar. Soon after a breeze getting up, the general took up his hat, and put it on, and then continued his parade between the mainmast and the cuddy. In time, the heat melted the tar, which began to stream down his cheeks in unequal lines, to the great amusement of all who beheld it, and were aware of the cause. Conceiving it to be merely the natural perspiration, he frequently lifted his hat to wipe his forehead, but without discovering the nature of the unguent. Finally, he went down to tea, and took his seat at table with the greatest gravity, when the bursting laughter of the company at length led to a detection of the trick. None laughed more heartily than his own volatile spouse; and in a little while he was able to enjoy the joke himself, though I must confess that, for the first five minutes, he seemed a little grave. Another of the passengers was a Scotchman, a captain of the Bombay Native Infantry, greatly given to the use of long pompous-sounding words, and whose wife, with good looks and good nature, was perpetually exciting the mirth of the company by silly remarks. There was nothing singular about the rest of the company.

We reached latitude 0 without a single adventure of the least consequence. In the morning of the day on which we were to gain that point, the last-mentioned lady asked if she could have a sight of the line through a telescope. A silk thread was fastened across the bottom of the glass, and she was desired to take the instrument into her own hands, and look out for it. She immediately exclaimed that she saw it; and after a time, having satisfied her curiosity, gave back the telescope, apparently quite contented.

We were previously made aware that on this day, according to ancient usage, the sailors were to be indulged in unrestrained licence, and that they were to employ the privilege in performing a well-known piece of mummery, in the course of which the passengers would be entirely abandoned by the master of the vessel as subjects for their uncouth and outrageous sport. I was not therefore surprised to receive in my cabin, before I had risen, a visit from the ship-armourer's deputy, a tall rough-looking fellow, with a countenance already inflamed above its ordinary red by an extra portion of grog. From his pocket he pulled out three thick pieces of iron, shaped like razors, which he laid upon the table. The edge of the first was jagged like a coarse saw; the next was somewhat less rough; and the third had comparatively a smooth edge.

"There, young man," said he, "which of these beautifully tempered implements of my trade—for I am the mighty Neptune's barber—would you prefer being used about the worst part of your fair-weather countenance —number one, two, or three? They are all admirable shavers, and will take off a beard like yours to a hair."

Alas, I had scarcely then a beard to my chin. "Why," I answered, in a tone of extreme modesty and good temper, "as you are so polite as to offer me a choice, I should much prefer the instrument with the smoothest edge."

"That razor," replied my visitor, "cannot be used upon mortal chin, unless the privilege of being shaved with it is well paid for. It is daily applied by me to the immortal face of my great master Neptune. You cannot of course expect to have the beard taken off yours with the same heaven-tempered article, unless you pay a handsome fee for the honour."

"Oh, very well," said I, and placed a guinea in his grimy palm.

"Nay, young gentleman, that is the price of number two. I never apply number three to the chin of a mortal for less than two guineas and a pint of rum."

I immediately gave him the two guineas and a bottle of brandy, with which he professed to be content.

This nautical Figaro now quitted me, and went to a young man in the steerage, who was on his passage to Bombay as a free merchant.

"Well, my fine fellow," said the royal barber, "how

G

do you find yourself in this here latitude? how's your beard? for you'll be shaved to-day, as sure as my name's Ben Bartlett. But don't mind; it will be done nicely, for you are in capital hands. Can you pay to be scraped genteelly, for you know we don't shave in this here latitude for nothing?"

"I have crossed the line before, so that I'm not a candidate for the honour you would confer upon me."

"When did you cross the line? You look too much like a land-lubber to have had my master Neptune's certificate of having passed his borders. Don't think to gammon older heads than that curly skull which wags so jauntily upon those spare shoulders."

"Do you doubt my word?"

"Words, Mr What-d'ye-call-'um, are a sort of coin that don't pass current in these here parts; we only take pieces with the king's head upon 'em. And as to your having crossed the line, you won't get any body on the other side on't to believe it. I must let you into a little bit of a secret. Our king, brother to the great Jupiter, but this very morning went up in a water-spout to the realms of old father Saturn, and looked over the register, kept in the Rolls Court of his dominions, to see who had paid the fee of passage over the borders of Neptune's empire, but he saw no such name as yours upon the rolls, and you know it must have been recorded had you crossed. Come, your money, or as sure as you've a beard upon your chin, it will be rasped with number one."

Thus ended the colloquy, and the poor young free merchant, who I verily believe had crossed the line two several times, having determined to resist the levy of the fictitious Neptune and his accessaries, was set down by the imperial shaver upon the list of candidates for the saw-edged razor.

To every passenger in both parts of the vessel, the delegate paid a similar visit. Some, who had crossed the line before, and were vouched for by the captain, escaped impost, but with difficulty, for this was a fact about which Neptune's officers seemed remarkably inclined to be sceptical. The Scotch captain was the only man in our cabin who neither substantiated a former passage nor submitted to the impost, and the barber left him with many ominous grumblings. After the round had been completed, and a register made, specifying the respective candidates for numbers one, two, and three, an order was given for the passengers to go below, in such a peremptory tone, that I really began to fancy that the command of the ship had been resigned to the counterfeit Neptune.

When assembled in the steerage, we were desired to wait there patiently until summoned upon deck into the presence of ocean's king. We had all taken care to dress ourselves in coloured cotton jackets and trousers, to avoid adding the sacrifice of a good suit of clothes to that of the coating of our chins. While stuffed under hatches, we heard the bustle of preparation above, and looked forward with feverish anxiety to the moment when the first of us should be summoned upon deck. It was really a painful state of anxiety, and I well remember to this day the extreme agitation I endured whilst under the torture of suspense. Some of the party affected to laugh at the thing as a good joke, but there was an expression on every countenance not to be mistaken, which explicitly told that it would turn out an agreeable joke to none.

I listened to the din overhead, and a rumbling noise soon convinced me that the mummery had begun. When it was ascertained that the ship was near the line, a loud shout was raised by the sub-marine aristocracy, arrayed in their official robes, and decorated with their respective badges. At noon, the presence of the mighty Neptune was announced by the blowing of a long tin horn from the forecastle. This summons was answered by the officer of the watch through a speaking-trumpet. The potentate of the deep was then drawn forward upon a gun-carriage to the quarter-deck, where the captain was ready to receive him. Neptune upon this occasion was personated by the ship's armourer, a tall strapping blacksmith, whose limbs were cast in a mould of Herculean proportions. He stood at least six feet three inches out of his shoes, and was altogether a fine fellow, possessing a coarse but shrewd and ready wit, and performing his part, in spite of deep potations of grog, in a manner by no means unworthy of the majesty which he represented. He bore in his hand a trident, the head of which, formed by his own ingenuity and labour, was fixed into the discarded handle of a mop. The car in which he sat was a water-tub, propped upon a gun carriage, and decorated with flags. He was drawn by eight sturdy seamen, in the character of Tritons. Neptune, round his capacious forehead, " the likeness of a kingly crown had on," being neither more nor less than an old tin kettle, the bottom of which had been thumped out, while the sides had been filed into spires, to resemble a diadem. The upper part of his body was naked, and painted a nondescript colour, between azure and green; several long strips of horse-hair hanging over his shoulders, and sweeping the edges of his triumphal car. His face was so bedaubed with paint, that not a feature could be recognised. His right hand held the trident; his left was stuffed most majestically into his breeches pocket.

As soon as the sea-god was dragged to the quarter-deck, the trembling victims of his tyranny were allowed for a short time to breathe a freer air. The hatches being uncovered, as many of us as could get on the ladder were permitted to take a peep at the farce that was going on. Neptune's Tritons were far more grotesque than their sovereign master, being so drunk that they could scarcely stand, and arrayed in such a manner as to make them appear as monstrous as possible. Their brows were encircled with wet swabs hanging over their shoulders, dripping with black bilge water, and spattered with oatmeal. Their faces were smeared with red ochre, the upper parts of their bodies being naked, and painted with the rude forms of dragons, whales, and " monsters of the deep."

Amphitrite, upon the present occasion, was represented by a short sturdy sailor, whose growth had stopped so long before his manhood, that he carried the height of a mere boy in the breadth of a vigorous man. He was dressed in a costume by which it was difficult to know to which sex the spouse of his aquatic majesty claimed to belong. Upon her head she wore what was intended for a wig, composed of hemp frizzled by the barber for the occasion; and down her broad back hung two dripping swabs, curled upon a marlinspike and covered with oatmeal, like those which encircled the foreheads of her attending Tritons. From her waist depended a coarse mat, which supplied the place of a petticoat, hanging to her heels, and thus concealing the muscularity of her royal legs. She stood by the side of Neptune with a pipe in her mouth, from which she propelled volumes of smoke.

At Neptune's left hand stood the barber, armed with his three razors, and a large brush fixed to the end of a broomstick. Neptune was no sooner placed upon the quarter-deck, than the captain advanced, made him a profound bow, and desired to know his pleasure. The potentate immediately drew from the bottom of the car a sort of chart and a pair of compasses. The former he placed upon his knee, and with the latter began to measure the boundaries of his empire, in order to show that the ship had reached the limits of that portion of ocean which was common property, and was about to enter those dominions over which the imperial son of Saturn especially presided, and into which he allowed no one to pass without paying a fee, and undergoing that divine rite of chin-scraping which should constitute him henceforward a free denizen of his sovereignty.

The captain acknowledged the truth of Neptune's representation, as well as the justice of his claim, and forthwith ordered the hatches to be again closed upon the passengers. We were all in a state of miserable suspense during the settlement of these preliminaries, and it became a question whether we should not, one and all, resist the tyranny with which we were threatened. By the majority, however, it was deemed imprudent to oppose a set of drunken sailors, sanctioned as their amusement was by the captain and officers of the ship; we therefore unanimously resolved to offer no opposition.

The summons at length arrived for one of the captives to ascend the deck, when the formidable barber, with his three razors, waited to receive him. This caused a general shudder, though some affected to laugh at what they called a good joke; it was, however, very evident that they really thought it a bad one. The hatches being opened, the surgeon, who, though a young man of firm nerves, did not at all approve of the ceremony, was first ordered to mount the steps: this he did with just that sort of alacrity which a criminal displays when going to be hanged. His eyes were bandaged, and as his motions were rather slow and reluctant, he was dragged by the arm through the hatchway by two stout Tritons, who exercised their rude jests upon us as we stood gaping at the unhappy victim about to undergo the infliction of number two. When he had reached the quarterdeck, the hatches were instantly closed upon us, and we were left to our meditations.

"Well, my lads," said the sailor who had been placed in the steerage to take care of us, " 'twill soon be over now, and when you've had your ducking, you'll be as frisky as the merriest of them. They don't take long a-shaving land-lubbers. I remember when I was scraped, the skin didn't fairly cover my chin again for six weeks, and I was all the while like a scalded pig, sore and tender."

This sort of bantering was continued until a second of the party was summoned into the presence of Neptune and his satellites. He ascended as reluctantly as the doctor, amid the coarse jeers of the Tritons, who, by this time, showed clearly that the grog had so mounted into their heads as almost entirely to deprive them of the command of their heels.

Four victims were summoned to the shaving-tub before I was called upon. When I heard my name announced, though I pursed up my features into a sort of careless grin, in order to show that I had no apprehension of what I was about to undergo, my heart knocked against my side with such energy that I could hear the pulsations. I ascended the steps without a murmur, and with as ready an activity as I could command. The bandage which had been placed over my eyes did not entirely obstruct my vision, and I could see downwards with tolerable clearness. Upon reaching the deck, I was conducted to an immense water-tub. Across a segment of its vast circumference, a plank was laid, on which I was immediately seated. Seeing that the barber, now so intoxicated as to be scarcely able to stand, was preparing to apply the roughest razor to my chin, I reminded him that I had purchased the privilege of being scraped with the smoothest. "You say true, my lad—I had forgot," he grumbled, with a lounge that had nearly cast him headlong on the deck, but suddenly grasping the side of the tub, he secured his footing. " I took you for the land-jack who pretended he had crossed the line, and refused to come down with the toll. When it comes to his turn, wont I harrow his face to a pretty tune!"

The compost with which he intended to besmear my chin was now placed in his hand. It consisted of tar, grease, and sundry other much more offensive simples. Having well filled the brush, he placed it opposite to my mouth, asking me at the same moment if I did not find him a very agreeable barber. The bandage round my forehead being by this time considerably loosened, I could distinctly see the brush, and being aware of the intention, kept my lips closed. I knew that, had I separated them, the brush and that villanous mixture with which it was charged, would have been instantly stuffed between, for the amusement of the drunken fellows by whom I was surrounded. As I did not reply, another question was asked; but at this moment, feeling the man stagger, I slipped from the plank upon which I was seated, and pushed from me the unsteady barber, who immediately fell upon his back. Before I could effect my escape, I was seized in the sinewy grasp of a Triton, and pitched head over heels into the tub. The moment I rose, I was pushed under water of a very foul quality, and this was continued until I was nearly suffocated.

The barber, meanwhile, was raised with some difficulty, vowing vengeance against me for having presumed to obstruct him in the performance of his honourable functions, and he certainly would have inflicted upon me the discipline of number one, had not the officer of the watch, with whom I happened to be something of a favourite, interfered, and saved my face from certain excoriation. I was at length suffered to escape with only a severe ducking, amid the murmurs of the disappointed barber.

No sooner had I quitted the tub, than the Scotch captain, by virtue of a privilege of the initiated, soused me from head to foot with a pailful of salt water, which, however, was rather agreeable than otherwise, as it helped to clean me. Anxious to witness the proceedings of the mummers, I seated myself on the poop, and beheld the remaining passengers one after another brought on deck, and subjected to the ceremony. The whole scene struck me as being disgraceful to a British ship's company. Every one of the crew who took part in the business, was so intoxicated that he could scarcely stand, and the blasphemies which they uttered were appalling. There was something in their frolics that savoured more of a savage spirit than of the supposed character of English seamen.

Among the last of the passengers summoned, was the young man who had so vigorously resisted the impost in the morning. He was dragged from the steerage with extreme violence, to which, contrary to my expectation, he offered no resistance. When seated upon the cross beam over the tub, having opened his lips to answer a question which was put to him, the horrid brush was instantly thrust between, to the infinite amusement of the onlookers. The barber then lathered his face up to the very eyes, all of which was borne with seeming patience. Emboldened by his tameness, which appeared like cowardice, the drunken monster then took up the deeply serrated blade, and, sweeping it smartly along his cheek and chin, inflicted several gashes, from which I could see the blood immediately begin to flow. Incensed at length by this cruel usage, the lad suddenly slid from the plank, tore the bandage from his eyes, and, striking the barber upon the forehead with his whole force, laid him flat upon the deck. He was immediately surrounded, but, seizing the trident from the grasp of Neptune, who was so stupified from intoxication that he could scarcely hold it, the ill-used youth wielded it with such lusty energy that he laid several of those who attempted to capture him beside their prostrate companion, the shaver. Having cleared his way through the hostile throng, he rushed towards the cuddy door, which, being locked in the inside, he burst open with a stroke of his hand, and proceeding to the captain's cabin, demanded admittance. This door was likewise locked, but with one blow of his foot he made a clear passage, and stood before the captain with his face begrimed and bleeding. "Is this," said he, in a tone of vehement indignation, "the manner in which you suffer your passengers to be treated? Sir, I hold you responsible for this indignity. I have been insulted and ill used by your men, and I here demand reparation from you for the injury."

The matter had now become so serious, that the captain thought it his duty to interfere. Instead of resenting the violence of his insulted passenger, he made him the humblest apologies, declaring that he never intended any portion of his crew should proceed so far as they had done, and immediately appeared in person upon deck, ordering that the men should offer no further molestation to the gentleman who had so justly punished them for their brutality. Thus harmony was restored, and the injured youth descended to the steerage to wash his begrimed features, and to plaster his chin.

When all the passengers had been shaved, that unhappy portion of the crew who had not crossed the line were brought upon deck to undergo the same operation. Each, as he was conducted to the tub, was stripped to the waist. A still more offensive mixture than that hitherto employed was made use of; and the manner in which some of the men were treated was really disgraceful to civilised beings, yet neither captain nor officer interfered to prevent the outrage. Several of the poor fellows quitted the deck with the tears streaming from their eyes, in consequence of the gashes inflicted upon their chins. One fine athletic man refused to permit the vile ceremony to be performed upon him, upsetting the imperial car, knocking down the drunken officials, and making his escape unharmed. He was however followed by a strong party of the crew, some of whom were less intoxicated than those immediately composing Neptune's train; these seized him, after a strong resistance, and forced him upon deck. Having fastened a rope round his waist, they hoisted him to the mainyard-arm, and let him drop from thence into the sea. Here they kept him until he was nearly drowned, and most probably this consummation would have been effected, had not the officer of the watch interfered, and insisted upon the man being drawn up. He was obeyed with much reluctance, and the poor fellow was laid upon the deck all but senseless. The matter did not end here; for the man being removed below, no sooner recovered from the effects of his cruel bath than he made his appearance among his drunken companions, and tearing off the swabs from Neptune's and the barber's brows, he seized each by the hair, and dashed their heads together with such violence that both fell speechless upon the quarterdeck. He then belaboured the drunken Tritons with such earnestness, that several fell prostrate beneath the might of his muscular arm. This created a general tumult, which was not allayed before more than one broken head had been committed to the charge of the surgeon. The champion in this affray finally retired without a scratch, for he had fortunately escaped the infliction of the razor.

Thus terminated these disgraceful proceedings. Many

of the landsmen were not subjected to the penalty of being shaved, in consequence of this opportune tumult, as the captain now interfered, and would not allow the sport to proceed further. Nearly all the men who had participated in it were in such a state of inebriation as to be unable to go below, but threw themselves under the forecastle, where they slept until the fumes of the grog were dissipated; though their bloodshot eyes and red inflated cheeks continued for days to mark the extent of their debauch.

Since this time, I have been informed, the ceremonies so long customary on crossing the line have fallen much out of observance, or have been greatly tempered. Perhaps one cause of this may have been a certain lawsuit which took place some years ago at Bombay. A gentleman who had taken a passage on board an Indiaman for that port, having heard that he would probably be subjected to the usual ceremony on crossing the line, remonstrated on the subject with the captain, from whom he demanded protection. The latter stated that he never interfered on these occasions—that it was an old custom, which he could not attempt to put a stop to—and, in short, that he could not save his passengers from the usual infliction. "Sir," observed the gentleman, "I have paid you handsomely for the use of a cabin on board your ship. Whilst I continue to occupy it, it is as much my house as a house would be for which I paid rent. No one has any right to enter it but with my consent, and I shall consider it sacred from intrusion whenever I may think proper to retire to it, as a protection against the assumed privilege of your crew. I shall neither pay them their demand, nor suffer them to intrude upon my privacy, on the day when you think proper to give them a licence to be tyrannical." "As you please," was the reply.

On the following day, Neptune hailed the ship, and the recusant individual, who had retired to his private apartment, was summoned to appear. He refused. The door was immediately tried, but found too strongly fastened to be forced. The man who officiated as barber on the occasion, and another man, were then lowered over the ship's side, and, entering the cabin by the port-hole, dragged the refractory malcontent through it, hauled him to the deck, and there subjected him to the rite in its severest and most disgusting form. Upon reaching Bombay, he brought an action against the captain, and recovered three hundred pounds damages.

ADVENTURE WITH A WHALE.

In an American tale, entitled " Miriam Coffin, or the Whale Fisherman," are found a variety of details relative to a wild class of beings—the fishermen of Nantucket, a seaport in the state of Massachusetts; among the rest is the following animated description of the chase and capture of a whale:—

The noble animal—for it was a right whale of the largest class—held on its course up the bay, scooping its food from time to time, and annihilating its thousands of small fish at a dive; leaving the boats far in the rear, and darting off in new directions, until those who were most on the alert, or rather those who pulled the most constantly, were fain to give up the chase, and to lie on their oars. Intent upon his prey, the whale appeared unconscious of the dangerous vicinage of the ships, and played among them with a temerity which evinced a tameness, or perhaps an ignorance of its danger, that plainly showed he had never been chased by the whaler, or hurt by the harpoon. The animal, gorged with its fishy meal, at last commenced its retreat from the bay; and the boats manœuvred to head him off as he retired. Obeying the instinct of his nature, he now showed his flukes, and vanished from the sight before the boats could get within striking distance. A calculation being made where he would next appear (for beneath the water the whale does not deviate from a direct line in his horizontal progress), a general race ensued; and each strove, as if life were on the issue, to arrive first upon the spot. Some twenty minutes' steady and vigorous pulling found the foremost boats a full mile behind the whale when he rose again to breathe. Several boats were unluckily ahead of Seth (of Nantucket) in the chase, as their position at starting enabled them to take the lead when the animal began to push for deeper water. But Seth's men had been resting on their oars, while nearly all the others had exhausted their strength in following the whale among the ships; and the captain judged rightly, that, in darting after his tiny prey, he would lead them all a bootless dance. He had determined to wait for the retreat, and then to hang upon the rear of the enemy.

There were others, however, acquainted with the soundings of the bay, whose tactics were scarce inferior to Seth's; and the advantage gained over him by several boats was proof of this, or at least of the superior accuracy of their calculations. It was a long time since Seth had given chase to an animal of the right whale breed; he had grappled of late only with the spermaceti; and therefore it was not to be wondered at, at this time, and in the circumstances, that some around him should beat him in manœuvring in the bay. But, in the steady chase, he knew that he could count upon the speed and bottom of his boat's crew, and he was now resolved to contest for the victory. " We have a clear field now, my boys—give way steadily—we gain upon them—give the long pull, the strong pull, and the pull all together—keep her to it—heave ahead, my hearties!" Such were the words of Seth, as, with eyes steadily fixed upon a certain point, and with his steering-oar slightly dipped at times, he guided the light whale-boat unerringly towards the place where he expected the whale to reappear. One by one he had dropped his antagonists by the way, until three only remained, manfully struggling between him and the prize. The whale again breathed at the surface, and the distance between the headmost boat and the animal was found to be diminished to half a mile, while the ships in the bay were run " hull down." The pursuers were now out upon the broad ocean. Those who had abandoned the chase in despair were slowly returning to their ships. The rigging of the vessels was manned by anxious spectators, watching the motions of the tiny specks out at sea with beating hearts. The whale again cast his flukes into the air, and sank from the view of his pursuers. Now came the tug of war.

"You must beat those foreigners ahead," said Seth to his men, "or crack your oars: they are of good American ash, and will bear pulling," continued he: "Give way with a will!—pull—pull, my lads; that whale will not sink again without a harpoon in his body; and 'twill never do to tell of at home that we allowed men of other nations to beat us. Keep your eyes steadily on your oars; mark the stroke of the after-oar, men—and give way for the credit of the Grampus!" Here Seth braced himself in the stern-sheets, seized the steering-oar with his left hand, and placed his right foot against the after-oar, just below the hand of the oarsman. "Now, pull for your lives!" said he, "while I add the strength of my leg to the oar:—once more!—Again, my boys!—once more—there—we pass the Spaniard!" "*Diabolo!*" exclaimed the mortified native of Spain. The additional momentum of Seth's foot, applied to the stroke oar, had done the job; but two more boats were to be passed—and quickly too—or all the labour would be lost. "At it again, my boys!—steady—steady—give way!—give way for the honour of the Grampus. One pull for old Nantucket!—and—there we have shown a clean pair of heels to the Dutchman!" "*Hagel!—Donder and blixem!*" said the Hollander. "There is but one boat ahead," said Seth; "it is the Englishman! We must beat him too, or we have gained nothing! Away with her—down upon him like men! One pull for the Grampus, my boys! another for old Nantuck——" The American now shot up alongside of the English boat; but the honour of the nation, too, was at stake; they bent to their oars with fresh vigour. Five athletic Englishmen, each with a bare chest that would have served for the model of a Hercules—with arms of brawn and sinew—swayed their oars with a precision and an earnestness that for a minute left the contest doubtful. The English commander, seeing how effectually Seth managed the stroke-oar with his foot, braced himself in a similar attitude of exertion, and his boat evidently gained upon the Nantucketer. Seth saw the increase of speed of his rival with dismay. The whale, too, was just rising ahead. The bubbles of his blowing, and of his efforts at rising, were beginning to ascend. It was a moment of intense anxiety. The rushing train or vortex of water told that he was near the surface.

Both commanders encouraged their men anew by a single word; and then, as if by mutual consent, all was silent, except the long, measured, and vigorous stroke of the oars. "For Old England, my lads!" shouted the one. "Remember old Nantucket, my boys!" was the war-cry of the other. Both plied their oars with apparently equal skill; but the hot Englishman lost his temper as the boat of Seth shot up again head and head with him, and he surged his foot so heavily upon the after-oar, that it broke off short in the rowlock! The blade of the broken oar became entangled with the others on the same side, while the after-oarsman lost his balance, and fell backward upon his leader. "I bid thee good-bye!" said Seth, as he shot ahead. An oath was vociferated by the Englishman. "Way enough —peak your oars!" said Seth to his men. The oars bristled apeak, after the fashion of the whale-fishermen. The harpooner immediately seized and balanced his weapon over his head, and planted himself firmly in the bow of the boat. At that instant the huge body of the whale rose above the surface; and Seth, with a single turn of his steering-oar, brought the bow dead upon the monster, a few feet a-back of the fin. Simultaneously with the striking of the boat, the well-poised harpoon was launched deep into the flesh of the animal. "Starn all!" shouted Seth. The boat was backed off in an instant; and the whale, feeling the sting of the barb, darted off like the wind. The well-coiled line flew through the groove of the bow-post with incomparable swiftness, and it presently began to smoke, and then to blaze, with the rapidity of the friction. Seth now took the bow with his lance, exchanging places with the harpooner, and quietly poured water upon the smoking groove, until it was cooled. The oars were again peaked, and the handles inserted in brackets fixed on the ceiling of the boat beneath the thwarts, the blades projecting over the water like wings; and the men, immoveable, rested from their long but successful pull: and much need they had of the relief, for a more arduous or better contested chase they had never experienced. The line in the tub was now well-nigh run out; and the boat-steerer, with a thick buckskin mitten or *nipper*, as it is called, for the protection of his hand, seized hold of the line, and, in a twinkling, caught a turn round the loggerhead, to enable the man at the tub-oar to bend on another line. The rapidity of the animal's flight the while was inconceivable. The boat now ploughed deeply and laboriously, leaving banks of water on each side, as she parted the wave, that overtopped the men's heads, and effectually obscured the sight of every object on the surface. The swell of the closing water came after them in a heavy and angry rush. The second line was now allowed to run slowly from the loggerhead; and a *drag*, or plank about eighteen inches square, with a line proceeding from each corner, and meeting at a point like a pyramid, was fastened to it, and thrown over to deaden the speed of the whale. Another and another drag was added, until the animal, feeling the strong backward pull, began to relax his efforts; and presently he suddenly descended, though not to the full extent of the slackened line. It now became necessary to haul in the slack of the line, and to coil it away in the tub carefully; while the men pulled with their oars, to come up with the whale when he should rise to the surface.

All things were soon ready again for the deadly attack. The ripple of the whale, as he ascended, was carefully marked; and when he again saw the light of day, a deep wound, close to the barbed harpoon, was instantly inflicted by the sharp lance of Seth. It was the death-blow. "*Starn all!*" was the cry once more—and the boat was again quickly backed off by the oarsmen. The infuriated animal roared in agony, and lashed the ocean into foam. The blood gushed from his spout-holes, falling in torrents on the men in the boat, and colouring the sea. The whale, in his last agony, is a fearful creature. He rose perpendicularly in the water, head downwards, and again writhed and lashed the sea with such force, that the people in the retreating boats, though ten miles distant, heard the thunder of the sound distinctly! The exertion was too violent to last long; it was the signal of his dissolution. His lifeblood ceased to flow, and he turned his belly to the sun. The *waif* of the Grampus floated triumphantly above the body of the slaughtered leviathan of the deep—and the peril of the hardy crew was over.

CRUISE OF THE SALDANHA AND TALBOT.

THE following attempt to describe a scene which it has seldom been the lot of man both to witness and to survive, will possess a melancholy interest from the associations with which it is connected. We will only premise, by assuring the reader that the narrative is perfectly authentic, and was penned in a communication to a friend in Edinburgh, in almost the very words here set down. Some of our readers, perhaps, may remember of an extract from it appearing in the Edinburgh newspapers of the time, being inserted for the purpose of allaying the fears of friends and relatives in that quarter for the safety of those whom common report had, not irrationally, consigned to a watery grave:—

Lochswilly, Dec. 10. 1811, H. M. S. Talbot.

At mid-day of Saturday the 30th ultimo, with a fair wind and a smooth sea, we weighed from our station here, in company with the Saldanha frigate of thirty-eight guns (Captain Pakenham, with a crew of 300 men), on a cruise, as was intended, of twenty days—the Saldanha taking a westerly course, while we stood in the opposite direction. We had scarcely got out of the loch and cleared the heads, however, when we plunged at once into all the miseries of a gale of wind blowing from the west. During the three following days it continued to increase in violence, when the islands of Coll and Tiree* became visible to us. As the wind had now chopped round more to the north, and continued unabated in violence, the danger of getting involved among the numerous small islands and rugged headlands on the north-west coast of Inverness-shire, became evident. It was therefore deemed expedient to wear the ship round, and make a port with all expedition. With this view, and favoured by the wind, a course was shaped for Lochswilly, and away we scudded under close-reefed foresail and main-topsail, followed by a tremendous sea, which threatened every moment to overwhelm us, and accompanied by piercing showers of hail, and a gale which blew with incredible fury. The same course was steered until next day about noon, when land was seen on the lee-bow. The weather being thick, some time elapsed before it could be distinctly made out, and it was then ascertained to be the island of North Arran, on the coast of Donegal, westward of Lochswilly. The ship was therefore hauled up some points, and we yet entertained hopes of reaching an anchorage before nightfall, when the weather gradually thickened, and the sea, now that we were upon a wind, broke over us in all directions. Its violence was such, that in a few minutes several of our ports were stove in, at which the water poured in in great abundance, until it was actually breast high on the lee-side of the main-deck. Fortunately but little got below, and the

* Two small islands lying to the north-west of the isle of Mull. Tiree formerly was celebrated for a marble quarry, and a fine breed of small horses.

ship was relieved by taking in the foresail. But a dreadful addition was now made to the precariousness of our situation by the cry of " Land ahead !" which was seen from the forecastle, and must have been very near. Not a moment was now lost in wearing the ship round on the other tack, and making what little sail could be carried, to weather the land we had already passed. This soon proved, however, to be a forlorn prospect, for it was found we should run our distance by ten o'clock. All the horrors of shipwreck now stared us in the face, aggravated tenfold by the extreme darkness of the night, and the tremendous force of the wind, which now blew a hurricane. Mountains are insignificant when speaking of the sea that kept pace with it; its violence was awful beyond description, and it frequently broke over all the poor little ship, that shivered and groaned, but behaved admirably.

The force of the sea may be guessed from the fact of the sheet-anchor, nearly a ton and a half in weight, being actually lifted on board, to say nothing of the forechain-plates board broken, both gangways torn away, quarter-galleries stove in, &c. &c. In short, on getting into port, the vessel was found to be loosened through all her frame, and leaking at every seam. As far as depended on her good qualities, however, I felt assured at the time we were safe, for I had seen enough of the Talbot to be convinced we were in one of the finest sea-boats that ever swam. But what could all the skill of the shipbuilder avail in a situation like ours? With a night full fifteen hours long before us, and knowing that we were fast driving on the land, anxiety and dread were on every face, and every mind felt the terrors of uncertainty and suspense. At length, about twelve o'clock, the dreadful truth was disclosed to us! Judge of my sensations when I saw the surf and the frowning rocks of Arran, scarcely half a mile distant on our lee-bow. To our inexpressible relief, and not less to our surprise, we fairly weathered all, and were congratulating each other on our escape, when on looking forward I imagined I saw breakers at no great distance on our lee; and this suspicion was soon confirmed, when the moon, which shone at intervals, suddenly broke out from behind a cloud, and presented to us a most terrific spectacle. At not more than a quarter of a mile's distance on our lee-beam appeared a range of tremendous breakers, amongst which it seemed as if every sea would throw us. Their height, it may be guessed, was prodigious, when they could be clearly distinguished from the foaming waters of the surrounding ocean. It was a scene seldom to be witnessed, and never forgotten! "Lord have mercy on us!" was now on the lips of every one—destruction seemed inevitable. Captain Swaine, whose coolness I have never seen surpassed, issued his orders clearly and collectedly when it was proposed as a last resource to drop the anchors, cut away the masts, and trust to the chance of riding out the gale. This scheme was actually determined on, and every thing was in readiness, but happily was deferred until an experiment was tried aloft. In addition to the close-reefed main-topsail and foresail, the fore-topsail and trysail were now set, and the result was almost magical. With a few plunges we cleared not only the reef, but a huge rock upon which I could with ease have tossed a biscuit, and in a few minutes we were inexpressibly rejoiced to observe both far astern.

We had now miraculously escaped all but certain destruction a second time, but much was yet to be feared. We had still to pass Cape Jeller, and the moments dragged on in gloomy apprehension and anxious suspense. The ship carried sail most wonderfully, and we continued to go along at the rate of seven knots, shipping very heavy seas, and labouring much —all with much solicitude looking out for daylight. The dawn at length appeared, and to our great joy we saw the land several miles astern, having passed the Cape, and many other hidden dangers, during the darkness. Matters on the morning of the 5th assumed a very different aspect from the last two days' experience: the wind gradually subsided, and with it the sea, and a favourable breeze now springing up, we were enabled to make a good offing. I have nothing further worth mentioning respecting ourselves, than that we anchored here this morning, all safe. Fortunately no accident of consequence occurred, although several of our people were severely bruised by falls. Poor fellows! they certainly suffered enough: not a dry stitch, not a dry hammock, have they had since we sailed. Happily, however, their misfortunes are soon forgot in a dry shirt and a can of grog. Now they are singing as jovially as if they had just returned from a pleasure cruise.

The most melancholy part of my narrative is still to be told. On coming up to our anchorage here this morning, we observed an unusual degree of curiosity and bustle in the fort; crowds of people were congregated on both sides, running to and fro, examining us through spy-glasses; in short, an extraordinary commotion was apparent. The meaning of all this was but too soon made known to us by a boat coming alongside, from which we learned that the unfortunate Saldanha had gone to pieces, and every man perished! Our own destruction had likewise been reckoned inevitable from the time of the discovery of the unhappy fate of our consort, five days beforehand; and hence the astonishment excited at our unexpected return. From all that could be learned concerning the dreadful catastrophe, I am inclined to believe that the Saldanha had been driven on the rocks about the time our doom appeared so certain in another quarter. Her lights were seen by the signal-tower at nine o'clock of that fearful Wednesday night, December 4, after which it is supposed she went ashore on the rocks at a small bay called Ballymastaker, almost at the entrance of Lochswilly harbour. Next morning the beach was strewed with fragments of the wreck, and upwards of two hundred of the bodies of the unfortunate sufferers were found washed ashore. One man—and one only—out of the three hundred, is ascertained to have come ashore alive, but almost in a state of insensibility. Unhappily there was no person present to administer to his wants judiciously, and upon craving something to drink, about half a pint of whisky was given him by the country people, which almost instantly killed him! Poor Pakenham's body was only recognised this morning amidst the others, and, like these, stripped quite naked by the inhuman wretches, who flocked to the wreck as to a blessing! It is even suspected that he came on shore alive, but was stripped and left to perish. Nothing could equal the audacity of the plunderers, although a party of the Lanark militia was doing duty around the wreck. But this is an ungracious and revolting subject, which no one of proper feeling would wish to dwell upon. Still less am I inclined to describe the heart-rending scene at Buncrana, where the widows of many of the sufferers are residing. The surgeon's wife, a native of Halifax, has never spoken since the dreadful tidings arrived. Consolation is inadmissible, and no one has yet ventured to offer it.*

THE DREADNOUGHT.

THE charitable institutions of London and its neighbourhood have long excited the admiration of foreigners, and with it a respect for the English national character. Of the various establishments of this nature which attract the attention of strangers, no one is perhaps so worthy of remark as an institution for the relief of sick and distressed sailors. We do not here speak of Greenwich Hospital, which is adapted for the residence of decayed mariners who have spent their lives in the king's service, but of the hospital-ship Dreadnought, once of 104 guns, and now lying off Greenwich. This floating wall of Old England, after years of service in the navy, has been converted into an hospital, under circumstances that do honour to all the parties concerned. It appears, that in the winter of 1818, a number of gentlemen subscribed to a fund for the temporary relief of distressed seamen who at that time

* By a contributor to Chambers's Journal.

were found in the streets of London. These gentlemen, finding the funds increase, appointed a committee, and at a public meeting it was determined that a permanent Floating Hospital should be established on the Thames. In consequence of this arrangement, the Grampus, a 50-gun ship, was fitted up and appropriated to the use of sick and diseased seamen only. In 1830, in consequence of numerous poor fellows not finding room on board, and many cases of sickness and misery being thereby unassisted, a representation was made to his Majesty's government, and the Dreadnought was immediately fitted up with every attention to the purposes of humanity. To the lasting honour of every subscriber, from his Majesty, through a long list of noblemen, merchants, officers, and others, down to Jack in the waist, be it recorded, that attention in sickness, and relief under misfortunes to which seamen are liable, are here extended to the wretched of *all nations*. A benevolence so universal might well be appreciated in the utmost corners of the world; accordingly, we find in the list of subscribers the monarchs of Russia, Denmark, Prussia, Sweden, Belgium, and Portugal, also the heads of mercantile establishments in America and the East and West Indies.

Those best acquainted with the peculiar character of seamen, know that they have habits distinct from persons employed on shore. From long contempt of dangers, Jack has an absence of thought for the morrow, and often seems to have no idea of the possible approach of wretchedness; and if it come, he bears its utmost pang—strips the last rag from his back for relief, rather than enter an hospital on shore. To meet this unaccountable prejudice against infirmaries on land, the Dreadnought offers all that benevolence can teach or humanity suggest. The establishment possesses experienced medical gentlemen, acquainted with diseases incident to climes which seamen visit—acquainted with the causes of protracted illness, or exhausted strength, to which they are liable from severe privations, long exposure to debilitating heat or benumbing cold. Even the results of abject poverty are relieved, and a balm for affliction is here presented to every comer of whatever nation.

The situation of the hospital-ship Dreadnought is well determined, being contiguous to the docks, and in the stream where accidents are of frequent occurrence. But, from any part between the mouth of the Thames and London Bridge, if a sick seaman present himself alongside, he is at once received and his case attended to. This facility of reception is of incalculable benefit, as thereby the funds are rendered more extensively useful, and the unfortunate sailor is sooner enabled to resume his duties. All this is worthy of a maritime nation which stands indebted for a great portion of its prosperity to its hardy and persevering seamen. From a statement recently published, it appears that the number of patients who have received relief and assistance from this excellent institution, amounts to 23,040, of all nations—in the navy, 1679; in the East India Company's service, 1767; in the merchant service of different nations, 19,594. The receipts during the year 1834 were £6788, 15s., and they were nearly equalled by the expenditure. The utility of this institution is acknowledged to operate beneficially in putting a stop to the practice of giving relief to impostors in the streets and in the vicinity of London. Few, indeed, now of those who assume the jacket, trousers, and tarpaulin hat, are seamen; and the public ought to be upon their guard accordingly. Innumerable instances of the value of the Dreadnought in saving sailors from death or serious distress in the metropolis, could no doubt be mentioned. Within the compass of our own knowledge, one striking case occurred, which may serve to illustrate the utility of the institution.

Jack Pether was the *beau-ideal* of a British sailor, brave, generous, and regardless of self. Returning to Portsmouth from a cruise in the Mediterranean, he was paid off along with a number of his shipmates, and on coming on shore, behaved as most of his class do under similar circumstances. It is now a number of years ago, yet we still think we see Jack rolling along in the gaiety of his heart, decked out in new jacket and trousers, a straw hat that afforded no shelter to his weather-beaten face, and a black neckerchief that yielded no protection to his throat. Jack had not been long in Portsmouth before he fell in with the captain of a merchant vessel on the outlook for hands to carry his ship round to Deptford. He had already secured a complement of assistants—half-and-halfers—'long-shore men, who might do well enough in fine weather, but knew nothing of combating with the elements. He now wanted one who could reef and steer, to keep all right; and so Jack Pether was exactly the man for his purpose. The bargain was hastily struck, all hands were summoned on board, and the Lively Nancy swung out of Portsmouth harbour before the impulse of a gentle breeze. Jack had not spent a day on board before he saw the nature of the crew, and he only hoped that a gale would not arise to frighten and render them useless. A storm, however, did arise. The breeze freshened to a gale, and the gale to a tempest. What was now to be done? Beechy Head, a dangerous promontory projecting into the Channel, was to be weathered, and there its lofty cliffs already loomed through the driving spray in the distance. In this dilemma, the heroism of the true British tar was exerted to the utmost. He saw that nearly all depended on himself. Regardless of every thing but duty, he faced the breeze night and day, standing at the helm, or ever and anon dashing forward to bend the sails or trim the vessel to the storm, and then flying as speedily back again to his post at the tiller.

By this extraordinary protracted exertion, Jack Pether had at length the satisfaction of not only weathering Beechy Head, but of carrying the Lively Nancy past the Goodwin Sands into the mouth of the Thames, which he entered triumphantly, so far as his feelings were concerned, but almost a wreck in his own person, from constant exposure on deck, and the fatigues he had otherwise undergone. All danger being now over, and the ship consigned to its moorings at Deptford, the reaction on Jack's frame became apparent. He was desirous of reaching the place of his nativity near Hampton, but this wish could not be gratified, or carried into effect. Sinking down in a state of fever and entire prostration of strength, he was taken alongside the Dreadnought, and, almost as unconscious as a corpse, was raised by tackle to the deck. He was now attended to in every way that kindness and skill could suggest. On being searched, he was found to possess a considerable sum, which was put aside for him on his restoration to health. Having a good constitution, it was soon renovated to a consciousness of all that was proceeding around. The surgeons were skilful, the nurses were kind, the accommodations were comfortable, and Jack could see that all was right.

The thought of *her* at Hampton Wick now came over his mind like the sunrise on a benighted traveller; it brightened on his heart till pleasure glistened in his eyes; and he would fain have left the ward before his strength was restored. In this his wish was counteracted; he was told that his friends might be written to; even the secretary, who chanced to be on board, would do this; and all were anxious to render him service. In the interim, the owners of the brig, having been informed by the captain of the services rendered by Jack Pether, presented him with a handsome acknowledgment of his merits, and an accompaniment in the shape of a pecuniary reward.

The time was now arrived when his health was restored. He walked the deck, talked with others on board of dangers past, and with a feeling of regret left the place where he had enjoyed so much hospitality. He received his chest, his tarpaulin bag, his tin-case of papers, and cash to the utmost farthing. Then stepping over the ship's side, he descended to a wherry, and was rowed ashore in health and strength to pursue his way to Hampton Wick by the Kingston coach, the well-remembered coach on which he had ridden when a boy. The town of Wandsworth, too, he recognised, the old steeple of the church, and many a cottage on the road; but when he came to the hill that overlooks the Thames, as it winds along to Hampton Court, and saw the village in which resided she of all womankind the best, of all most lovely, and of all most true, he felt the wish to dart at once into the vale, and chided the galloping four-in-hand for their tardiness.

Down the hill he glides, and waves his hat as he passes the sign of "The Jolly Sailors." He sees faces he had known before; he feels as entering the port of home, at least the port that held all he esteemed on earth. The coach passes Kingston market-place; he heeds not the stone on which King John was crowned. He does not observe that the bridge is built of stone in place of an old wooden structure raised on a hundred piles; it is enough that he is in the village of Hampton Wick. He sees his Mary at her father's door; he springs from the top of the coach, presses her to his heart, and believes he is the happiest being in the world. He sees not the gaping, laughing people around him; he can only see that she is more beautiful than ever; that her eye is brighter, that her smile is sweeter, and that her manner is more endearing. He does not know what to do; he has a thousand things to say, but not a word escapes his lips; he gazes in her face till she blushes, and then he clasps her again, imprinting a kiss in which his honest heart partakes of bliss unspeakable. At length the tumult of his joy subsides, and he can see and feel like those around. He shakes a dozen hands and gives a hundred nods before he pays the coachman, or receives his luggage. He enters the humble dwelling of his fair one's father, and finds all right. He can obtain employment on shore; the money he has saved will give him a start in life, and he shall be blessed with the partner of his choice. It was even as he wished.

Jack often tells the story of his voyage, as we have rapidly sketched it, and always ends with mentioning the generous treatment he received on board the Dreadnought, for which his and his Mary's united gratitudes are mingled with their prayers. Success attended their exertions. They still live, and enjoy the blessings that ever accompany honest industry, and have frequently declared their intention to act ever on the principles of the Dreadnought hospital-ship, which is that beneficent sentiment—" Peace and good-will towards all."

ROSS'S EXPEDITION.

THE twofold object of approaching the north pole and making the north-west passage—that is, sailing round the northern extremity of America, from the Atlantic to the Pacific—after lying long dormant, was revived in 1817, chiefly by Captain Scoresby and his son, who for many years followed the whale-fishing trade from Hull with enterprise and success. From the representations that were made, an expedition was fitted out to attempt the discovery of the supposed passage, but with no useful result. Betwixt 1817 and 1826, ten voyages and journeys overland took place, all at the public expense. They, however, produced nothing beyond hazardous enterprises and a few discoveries within the arctic circle. The government being at length tired of fitting out expeditions of this description, the project of another voyage was set on foot by Captain Ross, and his nephew Commander Ross, with the assistance of a private patron, Felix Booth, a rich merchant and distiller in London, who advanced £18,000 to purchase and equip a vessel to proceed upon the voyage.

The ship which was by this means engaged was the Victory, a vessel, it seems, unsuitable for the expedition. She was fitted up with steam-engine and paddles, but the enginery was very inadequate. She sailed from Woolwich, May 23, 1829. A second vessel, named the John, was taken to carry stores and provisions; but the crew of the John mutinied, and the Victory was allowed to proceed alone. On the 23d of July, the Victory reached Holsteinberg, a Danish settlement in

Davis' Straits. Captain Ross there purchased stores from a wrecked vessel, and the governor presented him with six Esquimaux dogs, afterwards of essential use in dragging the sledges. The Victory then stood to the northward along the coast of Baffin's Bay; and having reached the latitude of 74° 14' on the 3d of August, ran across to, and on the 5th reached the entrance of, Lancaster Sound. On the 11th August, he steered direct for the south-west side of Prince Regent's Inlet; and having passed Elvin and Batty Bays, saw the spot where the Fury had been wrecked in 1825. It had been one of Captain Ross's speculations to avail himself of the stores of the Fury, a vessel abandoned by Captain Parry, and it turned out decidedly successful. The following is his account of the wreck and her stores:—

" We found the coast almost lined with coal, and it was with no common interest that we proceeded to the only tent which remained entire. This had been the mess tent of the Fury's officers; but it was too evident that the bears had been making frequent visits. Where the preserved meats and vegetables had been deposited, we found every thing entire. The canisters had been piled up in two heaps; but though quite exposed to all the chances of the climate for four years, they had not suffered in the slightest degree. There had been no water to rust them, and the security of the joinings had prevented the bears from smelling their contents. On examining the meats, they were not found frozen, nor did the taste of the several articles appear to have been in the least degree altered. This was, indeed, no small satisfaction, as it was not our luxury, but our very existence, and the prospect of success, which were implicated in this most gratifying discovery. The wine, spirits, sugar, bread, flour, and cocoa, were in equally good condition, with the exception of a part of the latter, which had been lodged in provision casks. The lime juice and the pickles had not suffered much; and even the sails, which had been well made up, were not only dry, but seemed as if they had never been wetted. It was remarkable, however, that while the spun yarn was bleached white, all appearance and smell of tar had vanished from it. We proceeded now to the beach where the Fury had been abandoned, but not a trace of her hull was to be seen. We therefore returned on board, and made preparations for embarking a sufficiency of stores and provisions to complete our equipment for two years and three months, being what we expected to want on the one hand, and to obtain on the other. Yet all that we could possibly stow away seemed scarcely to diminish the piles of canisters, of which we embarked whatever we could, together with such flour, cocoa, and sugar, as we wanted, all that we took being in excellent condition. We had found the spare mizen-topmast of the Fury, and this was selected by the carpenter for a new boom, in place of one that we had lost. We also got some anchors and hawsers, together with some boatswain's and carpenter's stores, to make up our deficiencies." After selecting these and other stores, the Victory stood along the coast to the southward. It was here Captain Ross found the land, which he named Boothia Felix, but which seems rather to have been the imposing of a new name than making any discovery. Captain Parry had twice visited the same land before. The progress now made was but slow, for they had large masses and floes of ice, and contrary winds, to contend with, while their miserable engines could not help them onwards more than a mile an hour. Sometimes they had to make fast to an iceberg, and drift with it.

After this, Captain Ross passed along the coast southward for about 150 miles to the south of Cape Parry, but was obliged to bring up for the winter in what he was glad to consider a commodious harbour, and upon which, always rendering honour to whom it is due, he bestowed the name of Felix Harbour. Those critics who are still querulous of the captain's sayings and doings, and even yet advocate a north-west passage, here find fault with thus creeping along the coast. Having reached their winter home, the first step was to lighten the ship, then to throw overboard the unserviceable engines, and to make such arrangements and regulations for the winter as appeared to be proper. The lightening of the ship made it necessary to cut away the ice from around her, to allow her to settle at the natural line. She rose nine inches by the operation. The men then proceeded to build an embankment of snow and ice all around her, to shelter her from the cold. The upper deck was covered with two feet and a half of snow, which, after being trodden down into a solid mass of ice, was sprinkled with sand, and made like a gravel walk. A roofing over all was made from the spare sails of the wrecked vessel, the canvass sides being carried so low as to cover the sides of the ship down to the embankment of snow at the gunwale. The lower deck, which was the floor of the house, was covered with hot sand every morning, and scrubbed with sand until eight o'clock, the usual breakfast hour. Copper flues were placed round the apartment to carry off the vapour; iron tanks, with the open side downwards, were placed over the apertures in the upper deck, to receive the flues from the steam kitchen, oven, and other parts of the lower deck. By this plan the apartments were kept dry and warm. The system of comfort and economy within was as perfect as could be desired; and although the temperature without usually ranged so low as 37 *minus*, yet the men, if there were no wind, could take exercise, and make hunting excursions. When confined to the house, walking for some hours a-day upon the upper deck and beneath the canvass roof, was another mode of occupation towards keeping the crew healthy. Spirits were not served out, it being supposed that the use of them in these regions is conducive to scurvy; but the men had tea regularly every evening at five o'clock. They seem to have been unable or averse to muster a dramatic corps, but they had an evening school, which they attended with some degree of profit. Each Saturday night they were always allowed to dance, and to drink to sweethearts and wives. On Sunday, no work was performed, and the day was spent principally in religious observances.

They kept their first Christmas in these regions in due form; indeed, the minced pies and cherry-brandy from the Fury's stores enabled them to do this in the most appropriate manner. After Christmas they were amused by an unexpected visit from a tribe of Esquimaux, who, to the number of thirty, made their appearance upon the 9th January 1830. Miserable and forlorn as these people are, they were found by our voyagers to have some useful knowledge, and they showed provident habits. Some of them, and, as in Parry's case, one of them a female, could even give such lessons in geography as our travellers were glad to receive. They were acquainted with Winter Island and Repulse Bay. One man drew with a pencil several large lakes close to that part of the country—showed the spots where his countrymen were to be found—and assured the voyagers that the land might be crossed in nine days to the ocean. Captain Ross, it ought here to be mentioned, had it in his power to show gratitude to the schoolmaster, by rather a singular recompense. Tallapin, one of his instructors, had lost a limb by having been frost-bit, and the captain presented him with a wooden-leg, which he received with the most reverential gratitude and wonder at its suddenly, yet effectually, restoring to him the power of locomotion.

Commander Ross set out on a land expedition about the beginning of April. He was accompanied by the chief mate, Blanky, and two Esquimaux guides, with their sledges and provisions. The result of the journey seems to have been, that the commander and his party, having crossed an isthmus a little to the south and west of the ship, reached the ocean; whereupon, he says:—
"I concluded that we were now looking upon the Great Western Ocean, of which these people had so frequently spoken to us, and that the land on which we stood was part of the great continent of America." A second and third journey were undertaken by the commander towards the end of April. The commander, besides acquiring in augmentation of his stores, two musk oxen, now possessed himself fully of the geography of the

isthmus connecting the peninsula, now named Boothia, with that land which has been considered above as part of the great continent of America. The isthmus was found to separate Prince Regent's Inlet from the Western Sea. A fourth expedition made it certain that the extent of the isthmus was about fifteen miles in width, consisting of a lake, ten miles long, in the centre, and of five miles of land.

In place, therefore, of proving an inlet into the Western Ocean, the expeditions of Commander Ross showed that Prince Regent's Inlet was shut in by land; and it having been ascertained that the southern and western shores of the inlet were closed round with land, the next important point was to ascertain whether the land to the south of the isthmus was part of the continent of America. This could only be done by Commander Ross and his party tracing the western shore, and that again depended upon the limited quantity of provisions which they could carry with them. The matter of short allowance had to be well considered. It being generally agreed to persevere a little longer, Ross proceeded first to a projecting headland, which he called Cape Felix; then twenty miles farther, over hummocks, ice, and snow, brought them to another headland, which he named Victory Point, and which was found to be in lat. 69° 37′ 49″, and long. 98° 40′ 49″. They saw a still more distant point, which they named Franklin Point; the difference of latitude between which and the general line of the coast of America seemed barely one degree. The distance from Victory Point to Cape Turnagain is stated to be not greater than the space they had travelled from the ship— namely, 210 miles. But the commander was here obliged to desist, and to return. The party had hardly enough of provisions, even at a reduced allowance, to carry them back to the ship. Before quitting Victory Point, the travellers erected, in testimony of their visit, a cairn of stones, six feet in height, and they placed in it an account of their proceedings, contained in a canister, but with little hope that their brief chronicle would ever meet an European eye. During the months of August, September, and October, attempts were made to put to sea; but the season proving singularly unpropitious, and the ice forming early, it became evident that they were doomed to pass another winter upon the spot, and as much of the following summer as might expire before circumstances permitted of their liberation; they therefore once more commenced housing the ship, and building embankments, and they resumed all those practices and devices formerly used with so much success for passing the long dreary winter.

Second Year.—In April 1831, Captain Ross and his nephew, the commander, set off on an expedition towards the isthmus. The captain's object appears to have been to ascertain the height of the land above the Western Sea, the commander's to fix the position of the magnetic pole. It was presumed, on their leaving England, that the magnetic pole was in lat. 70°, long. 98° 30' west. The commander has fixed the spot at lat. 70° 5' 77", and long. 96° 46' 45" west; but in this there is a good deal conjectural and unsettled, and it may be stated that neither of the expeditions resulted satisfactorily. The ship became loose upon the 28th of August; but after various attempts to get her free, they began again, in October, to dismantle and make their winter preparations. This winter passed away much as the last.

Third Year.—In February 1832, the effects of the long seclusion and peculiar habits of the voyagers began to be too perceptible. An old wound in the captain's side now broke out with bleeding, a sure indication of scurvy; and the medical report bore that all the crew were much enfeebled. The purpose to abandon the ship and try the boats came to be entertained; and towards the end of April, they commenced carrying forward with the sledges a certain quantity of provisions and the boats. The labour of travelling over ice and snow was very severe, and made more so by the occasional wind and snow-drift. The final abandonment of the ship took place on the 29th May 1832.

After a month's fatiguing work, and every attempt at escape having been baffled, they had once more to fix themselves in winter quarters, which they did at Fury Beach, where they constructed a house thirty-one by sixteen feet, seven feet in the ceiling to be covered with canvass, and upon which they bestowed the name of Somerset House. Here they set the carpenter to work to repair the three boats remaining of the Fury. Upon the 1st of August, the ice unexpectedly broke up, and the travellers set off in the boats, in the hope of reaching Baffin's Bay before the departure of the whalers. The sudden setting in of the ice, however obliged them again to desist. They hauled the boats on shore, left them there, and, on the 25th of September, set out across the ice on their return to Somerset House, where they arrived, after a most toilsome and harassing march, on the 7th of October. They had still in store plenty of flour, sugar, soap, peas, vegetables, pickles, and lemon-juice; but of preserved meats there was not more than might suffice for another voyage in the boats during next season.

Fourth Year.—The death of that most important member of a ship's crew, the carpenter, cast a damp upon the party. He expired on the 28th February 1833. Want of employment—short allowance of food —the melancholy induced by the uniform waste, where snow and ice were the only elements, had the effect by this time of reducing the whole party to a more indifferent state of health than had hitherto been experienced. Mr Thom, the purser, and two of the seamen, were severely afflicted with scurvy. The monotonous and depressed state of existence into which they had thus fallen, is well expressed in the following passage:— " When snow was our decks, snow our awnings, snow our observatories, snow our larders, snow our salt, and when all the other uses of snow should be at last of no more avail, our coffins and our graves were to be graves and coffins of snow. Is this not more than enough of snow than suffices for admiration? Is it not worse, that during ten of the months in a year the ground is snow, and ice, and 'slush;' that during the whole year its tormenting, chilling, odious presence, is ever before the eye?"

But deliverance was at hand. They finally quitted Somerset House, Fury Beach, upon Monday the 8th July 1833, with their boats. They were detained for a short time at Batty Bay; but finding the ice to separate, and a lane of water to open out, they succeeded in crossing over to the eastern side of Prince Regent's Inlet. They then stood along the southern shore of Barrow's Strait, and upon the 26th of August 1833, they discovered a sail. Tantalising delays and disappointments ensued for a time, but they at length succeeded in making themselves visible to the crew of one of her boats, who speedily came to the rescue. " She was soon alongside," says Captain Ross, " when the mate in command addressed us, by presuming that we had met with some misfortune, and lost our ship. This being answered in the affirmative, I requested to know the name of his vessel, and expressed our wish to be taken on board. I was answered that it was the ' Isabella of Hull, once commanded by Captain Ross;' on which I stated that I was the identical man in question, and my people the crew of the Victory. That the mate who commanded this boat was as much astonished at this information as he appeared to be, I do not doubt; while, with the usual blunder-headedness of men on such occasions, he assured me that I had been dead two years. I easily convinced him, however, that what ought to have been true, according to his estimate, was a somewhat premature conclusion, as the bear-like form of the whole set of us might have shown him, had he taken time to discover that we were certainly not whaling gentlemen, and that we carried tolerable evidence of our being 'true men, and no impostors,' on our backs, and in our starved and unshaven countenances. A hearty congratulation followed, of course, in the true seaman style; and after a few natural inquiries, he added, that the Isabella was commanded by Captain Humphreys; when he immediately went off in his boat, to communicate his information on board, repeating that we had long been given up as lost, not by them alone but by all England.

As we approached slowly after him to the ship, he jumped up the side, and in a minute the rigging was manned; while we were saluted with three cheers as we came within cable's length, and were not long in getting on board of my old vessel, where we were all received by Captain Humphreys with a hearty seaman's welcome. The ludicrous soon took place of all other feelings; in such a crowd and such confusion, all serious thought was impossible, while the new buoyancy of our spirits made us abundantly willing to be amused by the scene which now opened. Every man was hungry, and was to be fed; all were ragged, and wore to be clothed; there was not one to whom washing was not indispensable, nor one whom his beard did not deprive of all English semblance. All, every thing, too, was to be done at once; it was washing, dressing, shaving, eating, all intermingled; it was all the materials of each jumbled together; while in the midst of all there were interminable questions to be asked and answered on both sides; the adventures of the Victory, our own escape, the politics of England, and the news which was four years old. But all subsided into peace at last. The sick were accommodated, the seamen disposed of, and all was done for all of us which care and kindness could perform."

The fate of Captain Ross and his crew had been long lamented in England, where it was universally believed that his voyage had terminated fatally. Of course, his reappearance along with his party was hailed with great rejoicing as a kind of resurrection from the dead. Their exertions and sufferings had been great; still neither he nor his men had any claim upon the government, who had not appointed them, or given its sanction, in any way whatever, to the expedition, but which had been throughout a mere private adventure. They became claimants, however. Their applications for relief were well received, and, in the tide of general sympathy, readily and liberally complied with. The men, by order of the Lords of the Admiralty, received double full pay until they finally abandoned the ship, and full pay after that until their arrival in England, amounting in gross to a sum of £4580. Captain Ross himself received £5000 by a vote of Parliament, and, along with his friend and patron Booth, received the honour of knighthood. The gunner and purser of the Victory were promoted to ships of the line; the medical officer was put in the way of being made full surgeon in the navy; and Commander Ross was appointed to a ship, and put upon full pay for twelve months, in order that he might at the end of that service receive the rank of post-captain. Add to all this, that Sir John Ross published his travels in a dear form by general subscription, whereby he no doubt expected to realise further remuneration.

Without calling in question the measure of reward bestowed on Ross and his party, we may be permitted to say, that the expedition produced no result of the least value, in the way of either geographic or general scientific discovery. It was a voyage which led to nothing. The question as to the existence of a north-west passage was still as far from being answered satisfactorily as ever, while, with reference to Captain Ross's expedition, the fuss which was made about it, not to speak of the silly manner in which it was dramatised and puffed, threw an air of ridicule over what ought to have excited feelings of a contrary nature.

A CRUISE IN THE BALTIC.

OF all the bodies of water which cover the face of the earth, that known by the name of the Baltic is about the most furious, when the wind gives it the smallest provocation. Not only does it toss its waves aloft into the air, like any other sea of greater magnitude, but currents setting in different directions from the shores which surround it, drive against each other with the rage of embattled hosts, and embroil the waters in a tremendous conflict, wherein the wave, no longer preserving its unbroken sweep, is split into a thousand antagonist columns, which rush together in unimaginable uproar.

One fatal October I lent myself to a scheme for crossing the Baltic, from Germany to the Swedish coast, in a crazy brig. The day was beautiful and calm on which we first embarked, the water smooth, the air elastic, and under such flattering auspices were we seduced into that treacherous sea. For a few days the wind blew gently from the east, and wafted us steadily towards our haven. On such occasions a sea voyage is attended with infinite delight, and nothing can exceed the buoyancy of spirits which is felt by all. Smiles and good humour enlightened every countenance, and the rude tars were merry as they heaved the log, or drew yet more astern the stunsail sheet. But, alas, for the insecurity of human hopes and marine adventures! One night, the sun sank amidst those lurid and fleecy clouds which the sage pilot knows full well betoken a furious wind. Two hours after midnight the storm burst upon us, sweeping a perfect hurricane from the west directly in our teeth. A few hours more would have carried us into the Sound's still waters, and in a vain attempt to double a rocky promontory on the Swedish coast, our captain persisted for three days in exposing us to the fury of the storm. We tacked and tacked again, made short-legs and long-legs, all to no purpose. No headway was gained, and we at length yielded from the contest, and, turning our backs to the wind, scudded with a few stitches of canvass before it. Our object was to obtain shelter at the nearest point; and unless we returned to some port on the continent, none offered itself but anchoring under lee of the island of Bornholm, which lies in the middle of the Baltic. Under the high lands of this island was an open roadstead, and so long as the wind blew in the direction in which it had commenced, there was a safe and quiet anchorage. As it was, we had scarcely an alternative, and the destruction which a sudden chopping round of the furious blast would inevitably produce by dashing us on the rocky coast, was less regarded than the immediate peril which threatened a further exposure to the storm. When we had turned the northern angle of the island, we came again into smooth water, the ineffable luxury of which can only be appreciated by those who emerge from the hurly-burly of a tempest. Sliding gently along the eastern side of the island, we at length dropped our anchor amidst several other vessels driven there by the same necessity.

The next morning the boat was lowered for an excursion on shore. Although the wind was still blowing with unabated violence, so completely were we sheltered from its influence, that the water around us was scarcely rippled, and on the sloping banks of the island all seemed repose and quiet. Two little villages with their white cottages were in view, and on the summit of the hill the ruins of some ancient castle still frowned upon the plains below. Upon reaching the land, we made for the village which stood nearest our berth. Some young girls, whom we disturbed drawing water from a well, fled upon our appearance with marks of terror on their countenances, and took refuge in the houses. When we entered the village, we found only a few old men and women, whom our aspect did not scare into flight, as the more youthful population ventured only an occasional peep from the doorways, doubtless considering us as some terrible monsters escaped from the deep. As the Danish language is spoken upon the island, we were unable at first to hold any intercourse with the people around us; but at last a person in a somewhat better garb than his neighbours, advanced towards us, and, in the German dialect, invited us into his mansion. This we found to be the hotel of the village, and its occupier, as he himself positively assured us, the greatest man in the community. Though his house or cottage was upon a small scale, and as to furniture very bare, yet it was clean and orderly. It was, however, the most sumptuous abode in the parish, save that of the priest, who, our landlord informed us, lived about two miles up the country, in a very stately and magnificent residence. He likewise gave us to understand that he was the only individual in the place who ate mutton to his dinner on certain days in the week, his fellow-citizens living upon fish and barley bread the whole year round. "Yes," said he, "all the people look up to me except on Sundays, when the priest comes down to preach. Ah! he is a great man that priest. But I have seen much of the world also. I have been three times in Elsinore, and once in Rostock; and few can say as much. Yes, upon my word, I have seen a great deal —so much, that the governor himself sometimes asks my opinion when he comes this way. And he is a greater man than the priest!" As he thought that some doubts might still remain in our minds as to the importance he assumed, he proceeded to direct our attention to the articles of furniture in the two rooms he occupied, which, although of the most ordinary description, were in his eyes evidences of a superior luxury. Of his bed he seemed singularly proud. "See that bed," said he; "it is indeed a very fine bed. I assure you it is all stuffed with wool. But," added he with a sigh, "it is, after all, not so grand as the priest's bed."

Having thus, as he imagined, completely elevated himself in our estimation, he brought forth a bottle, and insisted upon our tasting such schnaps as never was known in Bornholm before. As an additional recommendation, he stated that the priest himself often took a glass of such an inestimable fluid, pronouncing it in the first order of things. Having therefore taken a sip of his cordial, which was similar to the common brandt-wein of Germany, and praised it in sufficiently high terms, we solicited some information from him as to any thing curious or wonderful which was to be seen in the neighbourhood. "There is the church," said he, "which is very, very old; and there is the priest, who is the most learned man that ever was known. He is the only man who knows when the church was built. As for the clerk, who lives close by, he is a miserable person, who knows nothing, though he pretends to tell all about it. Therefore you must not believe one word he tells you, for the fellow can jabber a little German. But I will accompany you myself." With these words, he led the way towards the church, which, although a small building, was evidently of great antiquity. Having readily found the clerk, who seemed the custodier of the edifice, he, with every symptom of alacrity, acceded to our request to enter and inspect it. With a species of flourish he drew forth a large key, and, opening the door, invited us to follow him. We found the interior in every respect similar to a church in some retired rural parish of England. What imparted to this ancient building an air of singularity, was about fifty mouldering banners, which hung down from the ceiling, and formed a sort of canopy along the whole extent of the church. Seeing that we regarded these trophies with a great degree of curiosity, the clerk put himself in the attitude of a man about to impart some important information, and, stretching his hand a little upwards, he thus commenced:—" The old and venerable relics which you now behold, belong to an age long since past. They represent to you, gentlemen, the arms and escutcheons of the famous Hanse Towns, which many a long year ago possessed this great and flourishing island. Here, also, are some of the banners of the glorious order of St Mary of Jerusalem, otherwise called the Teutonic Knights, who, they say, first brought Christianity amongst us. The sovereign of Denmark, who extirpated all these people from the face of the land of Bornholm, nevertheless gave his gracious permission to preserve these records of times and powers passed away, and we, who are deeply versed in history, can appreciate the magnanimity of such a resolution. But the people of the island are sunk in an ignorance not to be imagined." During the delivery of this oration, which was given in a sufficiently pompous manner, and apparently in the style of a man who repeats what he himself does not exactly comprehend, our friend of the schnaps shop gave sundry tokens of the impatience with which he listened to the effusion of the erudite clerk. " Gentlemen," said he, with infinite rage in his looks, " this scoundrel has learned all these fine things from the priest. You dare not deny it, sir; you cannot read two words in a book. Ignorance! do you compare yourself to me—me who have been thrice in Elsinore, and once in Rostock? Did I not recommend you to the priest? Do you not owe every thing to me—do you not owe me for a bottle of schnaps?" This last question seemed to bring down the unfortunate clerk from his airy flight, for he replied in a very subdued tone of voice, " Yes, yes, the priest taught me all this, but I saw no harm in repeating it." " Ah! there—I told you so," said the other, turning to us; " nobody knows any thing but myself. It is necessary, I assure you, to keep all these people in good order." The irascibility of this man of knowledge being now in some degree appeased, his feelings seemed to take an entirely new turn, in which a wish to promote the interests of his compatriot was predominant. Taking us aside, he represented to us the necessity of giving the poor clerk something to recompense the trouble he had bestowed upon us, and he himself kindly offered to convey any douceur which we should destine for him. We, however, thought it best to give the reward into the man's own hands, and we left the couple in eager discussion within the porch as to its proper distribution.

As we sauntered from the church, the clerk overtook us out of breath. " Gentlemen," said he, " the priest is exceedingly fond of strangers, and I am sure he will be displeased with me if I do not conduct you to his house. I trust, therefore, you will allow me to do so." As we had heard so much of this clerical personage, we had every inclination to accede to the learned clerk's offer. We therefore set off, and in about half an hour reached the parsonage, which was a one-storied house standing in the midst of a garden, not in the very best of order. To the clerk's inquiry whether the priest was at home, a girl in a blue flannel gown and wooden shoes directed us into a back court, where his reverence was at that particular moment killing one of his pigs. "Halt a moment," said our conductor; "let us wait till he has finished." We therefore stopped and contemplated the personage before us. He was a man of middle stature and robust make, quite a parson Trulliber in appearance, though not in character. His countenance was fair and ruddy, betokening perfect health. He had on neither coat nor waistcoat, and his striped shirt was tucked up above the elbows, so that his arms were nearly bared. A woollen nightcap hung down one side of his head, and from his ears were pendant two large brass rings. When disengaged from the operation in which he had been employed, he turned round and beheld us, whereupon he instantly stepped forward, and, seizing hold of the tassel of his nightcap, laid bare his cranium, and made us a profound bow. "I suppose, gentlemen, you are from the ships I see at anchor near the island. I am glad to see you. Pray walk into the garden for a few minutes, until I can appear to welcome you in proper form. You, Petersen," added he, addressing the clerk, "go and stir that blood until I send some one to relieve you." With these words, he retired into the house. The worthy priest was not long at his toilet, for he soon rejoined us in very spruce habiliments. "I am sorry this is not a gala day with us," said he; "but if you can eat oats and eels, I shall be delighted to entertain you at dinner. Yesterday we finished the last piece of mutton that was in the house, and it will be next week before we get any more. As to that pig," added he, smiling, "it is not for my own table—it goes off to-day to the garrison at Eartholm."

We immediately accepted his invitation, however oddly the viands sounded in our ears. He led us into the house, and presented us to his wife, who received us with great good nature. She was dressed in a very homely manner, and was evidently not accustomed to a life of sloth and luxury. The room we were ushered into was of the very plainest order. No carpets, stuffed chairs, or sofas, were visible. The good lady of the house assisted in arranging all things for the forthcoming feast. The functionary of the church himself lent his voice in suggestion or command as occasion needed ; and when at length a bowl smoking hot was brought in, he summoned us to the board. The dish we were called upon to discuss was composed of rancid eels, sunk in a sort of thick oat porridge, mixed up with hog's lard or some other potent unguent, a portion of which we got through in tolerable style, all things considered. We, however, resisted with a modest firmness the kind endeavours of our host to heap our plates with any further quantity, and preferred a glass of his small wine. During the repast, the good-hearted priest entertained us with some home sketches. "You see," said he, " I am not a man given to luxurious feeding, but I preserve my health and pass my days happily. Although, in the estimation of you men who mix in the world, I am poor and needy, yet by my parishioners I am considered as rolling in wealth. My stipend from the king is about £15 sterling, and I have a farm, for which I pay no rent, and which I cultivate myself. Upon this I keep my family, though the land is amazingly barren. But the people all regard me as the greatest man in the world, whilst I do my best to assist them in their sickness and poverty. They are principally fishermen ; but unless they fall in with ships at sea, they seldom find a good market for their commodity. They respect me not only as the wealthiest person in the district, but, I trust, also as their pastor. I preach to them every Sunday, and they gather from all parts to hear me. I thus live honoured by the people around me ; and as I am contented with my lot, I write myself down a happy man. One wish alone annoys me. I confess I listen sometimes to the voice of ambition. I would, gentlemen, be an historian—the chronicler of the great events of which this island has been the scene. I would withdraw from oblivion the names of the mighty men who have figured in its annals, and while I gained for myself infinite renown, I would approve myself a patriot zealous for the glory of his native land. Yes, gentlemen, such things come across me sometimes." And here he laid his hand upon his forehead, and preserved a deep silence for some minutes.

Whilst his reverence had thus lost himself in a glorious reverie, we took the opportunity of rising preparatory to our departure, which instantly brought him back to the material world. He insisted upon accompanying us back to our boat; and loading poor Petersen, the clerk, with bottles of fresh milk and a basket of eggs, he gave us good cause to recollect his kindness. When we reached the shore, he bade us a hearty farewell, and we parted with mutual good wishes for all that this earth can give of happiness and prosperity. The following day the storm having somewhat abated, we weighed anchor, and soon left the island of Bornholm—a land reckoned by its own simple-minded inhabitants the greatest in the world, but which, to our gaze, soon became a speck on the horizon, and hardly obtains a notice in the map of Europe.

NARRATIVE OF THE DEE, A MISSING WHALER.

THE DEE sailed from Aberdeen on its northern whaling expedition, on the 2d of April 1836, having on board a crew of thirty-three persons, including officers, and commanded by Captain Gamblin. The ship was freighted with the usual quantity of provisions, and possessed a most attentive surgeon in Mr Littlejohn. Having sailed northward, sixteen additional hands were taken on board at Stromness in Orkney; and thence proceeding to Davis' Straits, ice was reached on the 15th of May.

Being thus arrived near the fishing ground, preparations were made for capturing any whales which might make their appearance. The hopes of the crew, however, were in this respect baffled. For two or three weeks the weather was rather unsteady, and the progress of the vessel was considerably obstructed by loose ice and icebergs. On attaining latitude 66°, the icebergs were so numerous and dangerous, that serious fears were entertained for the safety of the vessel. After some delays, North-East Bay was gained, and the vessel was allowed to proceed as far as Frow Islands. An attempt was then made to move forward in a westerly direction, but the difficulties in this quarter proved so formidable, that the course was changed to about east-north-east, and, after several days' sailing, the Dee was fortunate enough to reach the north water in safety, accompanied by the Swan of Hull, and ten other vessels. Captain Gamblin now steered for Pond's Bay (on the west coast of Baffin's Bay), where he arrived on the 12th of August, without having encountered any material obstruction, one heavy patch of ice excepted. On the 13th, the first whale was seen, and the weather being fine, it was easily struck and secured. The fish were found to be plentiful in Pond's Bay, and, during the remainder of the month, other three were killed, and three dead ones picked up. The Dee then moved a little to the south, but was necessitated to return, having met with very heavy ice, and seen no fish. A number of vessels were at this time in Pond's Bay, one of which, the Friendship of Dundee, had been fortunate in killing fifteen whales. Finding the fish to be getting scarce, and the season being well advanced, Captain Gamblin thought it prudent to return homeward. He had gone but a short way, when he fell in with the Grenville Bay, the captain of which stated that he had tried a passage to the east, and had found it impracticable from the ice. It was now the 13th of September, and the crew of the Dee, beginning to entertain serious fears, went on short allowance. The captain then resolved to try the north passage, and succeeded in getting as far as 75°, in company with the Grenville Bay and the Norfolk. Cape Melville (on the north-east coast of Baffin's Bay) was now in sight; but the bay ice was "making too strong" to admit of further progress, and, after a consultation, the three vessels, on the 20th of September, bore away to the south. On the 23d, they were in latitude 71°, with heavy bay ice around them. Here they fell in with the Thomas and the Advice, of Dundee, which had also made an unsuccessful attempt to find a passage along the north-east coast, and had discovered that eight other vessels at least must have done the same, from the marks of as many ice-anchors seen on an iceberg. On the night of the 23d, the five ships had to be fastened, for greater security, to blocks of ice, called sconce-pieces. The three following days were spent in fruitless endeavours to find an opening to the south.

Though the weather had all along been rather easy, it appeared now but too plain to the unfortunate seamen that the ice surrounded them on all sides. They submitted to a further reduction of allowance, three pounds of bread a-week, with a proportionably small quantity of other provisions, being their mess. Again the five captains, after due deliberation, bore away to the north. On the 1st of October, the weather had become bad, with east-north-east winds, and snow, strong ice, and a heavy swell. Signals were once more hoisted for a consultation; but the Dundee vessels, though at this time in sight, did not observe the call. The determination come to by the other vessels was, to move as far south as possible for a wintering station. The failing of the wind, however, kept them nearly in the same place; and on the 8th, the whole five vessels were fast locked in ice, within sight of each other, in latitude 73° 12′, at the mouth of Baffin's Bay. On the 10th, it was found that the drift had carried them two and a half miles to the south, the wind being from the north and north-east. At this time the ice was so strong that the men could pass between the ships; but in the immediate locality of the Dee, the swell caused frequent and dangerous disruptions.

From this date, the peculiar sufferings of the crew of the Dee may be said to have commenced. Their allowance remained the same, but, from the scarcity of fuel, their beds became wretchedly damp. At first, to preserve the health of the men, and to keep their shivering bodies in heat, the most praiseworthy precautions were taken. A variety of exercise was allotted to them, such as the unbending of the sails, unshipping the rudder, and other toils, of no utility now, unhappily, to the ship. But the crew of the Dee had not long to resort to unprofitable labours to maintain the vital warmth of their frames. Notwithstanding the increasing hardness of the frost, the ice still remained in a loose state, and a fatal crush on the ship became the subject of continual alarm. On the 16th, the latitude was 72° 50', wind strong, and large icebergs floating past. The ice began to press hard, and on the night of the 16th, the vessel was crushed up till it hung by the quarter, the ice squeezing all along as high as the guard boards. At daylight, all hands were called up to get out the provisions. At 8 P. M., the wind fell off, but the ship still hung by the quarter. The ice, however, was at rest till 11 P. M., when there was another dreadful crush, which passed off with less harm than could have been anticipated. On the 18th, the ice gave way in several places, and opened up so far that a warp had to be got out to secure the Dee. The other vessels, meanwhile, lay comparatively undisturbed. On the 20th, the ice closed again, with some severe squeezes, around the Dee. To strengthen the ship, its casks were placed in a peculiar way, and ten strong beams put in aft. This was done most seasonably, for, shortly after, two successive shocks took place, within half an hour of each other, of such tremendous severity, that the crew fled to the ice with their bags, chests, and every thing that could be lifted, under the impression that all was over with the timbers of the Dee. The sufferings of the night that followed were awful. Without fire, or shelter from the biting elements, the crew lay on the ice, gazing on their reeling and groaning vessel, while around them were extended vast fields of ice, studded with icebergs towering to the clouds, and threatening destruction to

J

all that came in the way of their motions. Miserable as their position was, the crew could not go on board for two days, during which time the ship experienced crushes still more severe than formerly. On the 22d, the men went on board to take out the remaining provisions, but had again to fly for their lives. The ice, however, fell quiet on the same night, and they again took back their provisions to the ship. On the 23d, a good many lanes opened up in the water—a most discouraging prospect, for this was always the time of greatest peril. Once more the crew took to the ice, and, by cutting the nearest parts into small pieces, cleared the vessel a few feet. The men then went for a few hours to rest, but were roused by another crush —the signal that their labours had been in vain. On the 24th, the ice broke up to a considerable extent, and the crew managed to heave the Dee backwards for a hundred yards, to a point where the ice seemed to be thinner. Great difficulties were experienced in again getting on board the chests and other articles, but at length every thing was replaced.

Warned by late dangers, and fearful of the wind, which blew from the most unpromising quarter, the north-east, Captain Gamblin resolved to cut a dock for the Dee. This was effected by the crew, aided by several men from the Grenville Bay, by means of heavy ice-saws, driven through the ice, as piles are sunk into the earth, and afterwards moved up and down by the men. In working the ice-saws, the crew suffered terribly from the frosting of their feet, consequent upon their standing in water. The Dee, when stationed in the cut dock, seemed to be in comparative safety. From the 26th till the 29th, the crew were chiefly employed in dragging ice in boats from the nearest bergs, to dissolve into water—the ice of the bergs being fresh. As the nearest berg was three miles distant, the severity of this labour may be imagined. A bear had been seen on the 26th, and on the 30th other three were seen and fired at, but without effect. Indeed, two of the men had a narrow escape from the animals.

Though comfort is a word that can scarcely be applied to the situation of the Dee's crew—placed in a latitude of 72° 50'—subsisting, to the number of forty-nine men, on a miserable pittance of provisions—with beds freezing, and little or no fire to dispel the cold—yet the position of the whalers on the 1st of November may be termed comparatively comfortable. The ice was firm around them, and the men might hope not to be overwrought, as well as underfed. Alas! things did not long remain thus. On the 2d of the month the dock gave way, and the ice again threatened to crush the vessel to pieces. This sad reverse did not overcome Captain Gamblin's firmness. He again got assistance from the Grenville Bay, and also from the Norfolk, and cut a new dock, in which, with much difficulty, the Dee was got moored. On the 3d, 4th, and 5th, the weather was very boisterous and snowy, and the sufferings of the crew were very great, their supply of coals being nearly exhausted. One boat was broken up for fuel, and another soon followed. On the 6th, the dock again gave indications of rending, and at night the destruction of the ship seemed so inevitable, that the men had to leave it. By an observation taken, it appeared that the Dee had drifted with the surrounding masses from 72° 50' to 72° 23'. Provisions were further reduced on the 7th, and on the 8th and 9th great fears were entertained of a crush. Several of the men were severely frost-bitten in the face, which was relieved by rubbing the parts with snow. A new dock was cut on the 10th, and the ship rendered a little more secure. A bear and two foxes were seen, but made their escape, to the great disappointment of the men, who longed to taste fresh food. What a delicacy even fox-flesh would have been, may be conceived from the fact, that the tails of the whales on board were cooked and eaten with great relish by the men.

A great advantage at this time was derived by the crew from a yard of canvass, given to each of them by the captain, and made into boots with wooden soles. Consolation, also, of a higher nature, was not wanting to the distressed mariners. On Sunday the 13th, Mr Littlejohn, the surgeon, at the request of almost all on board, began to read sermons and prayers—a duty frequently repeated afterwards, on week-days as well as Sabbath-days. The worship offered up by the crew was simple but sincere, and deeply consoling to themselves. The daylight had been for some time gradually becoming weaker, and on the 15th the sun was not visible—a thing novel to all on board, and rendered more depressing in its influence on their spirits, by the threatening appearance of the ice, which the wind and the current, called the north-east water, still continued to keep in dangerous motion. An observation of the 16th, showed the ships to be in latitude 71° 57'. Up till the 30th, nothing occurred worthy of observation, excepting the great change, beginning to be visible, on the healths of the men. Coughs, swelled limbs, and general debility, with small red discolourations on the skin, sharp pains and stiffness, were the common symptoms. Two foxes, killed on the 3d of December, gave hopes that fresh provisions might yet be got in considerable quantities; but these hopes turned out fallacious. On the 5th, the latitude was found to be 71° 12'—showing the drift to be still continuing.

On the 12th, when the frost was very severe, and the daylight nearly gone, the Thomas of Dundee, which lay farthest of the five ships from the Dee, was almost heeled over by a heavy pressure of ice, and the men reduced to a sad condition. On the 13th, the Thomas was a total wreck. Two of the crew died on the ice— the first deaths that had taken place. With great toil and hardship, the provisions were carried from the wreck by the men of the Dee and Advice, and were subsequently distributed, as were also the sailors of the Thomas, in equal divisions among the remaining ships. Unfortunately, the wrecked ship was too far off to supply firewood. Three days were spent in this labour, and the cold and wet to which the seamen were exposed in performing it, laid the seeds of that disease which now began to show its fatal power. This disease was scurvy, and it was marked chiefly by an excruciating pain in the mouth, and swelled gums, rendering eating a torture. On the 18th of December, twenty-one men were affected with scurvy. To add to their distress, the ice again gave way, and threatened to crush every one of the miserable vessels. The Advice and Grenville Bay were in greatest danger, and the crews were at times expectant only of death. The allowance of pork was reduced, on the 24th, to half a pound a-day for each man. Some of the men of the Dee were now so bad with scurvy as to be confined to bed.

The 1st day of January 1837 was a day of sorrowful remembrance, it being customary for the sailors of whaling vessels to be at that period in the enjoyment of all the pleasures of home, in the bosom of their families. On the 2d, 3d, and 4th, scurvy was making rapid strides among the Dee's men; fresh provisions, the only cure for the complaint, being out of the attentive surgeon's reach. On the 5th, the men applied to Captain Gamblin for an increased allowance of provisions. This he declined to grant, expressing at the same time his hope that they knew their duty better than to use force, which might certainly procure them their wish. To their credit, the crew disclaimed all desire to employ coercive means, and the gratified commander rewarded their forbearance, by giving each man a little additional flour to his mess. On the 6th, a brilliant sky gave hopes of the sun's speedy reappearance, and a large sheet of water on the starboard brought anticipations of release to the ships. A sad damp was thrown next day on these prospects, by the greater number of the crew of the Dee being unable to leave their beds, which were in a deplorable state from the intense cold, and also from vermin. On the 11th, the first death in the Dee took place, the sufferer being William Curryal, of Stromness. The funeral-prayer was read over the body by Mr Littlejohn, and the crew then, with hearts full of inexpressible sadness, carried it to a distant opening in the ice, where it was consigned to the deep. The daylight was now showing signs of return, and on the 16th, the sun, a joyful spectacle, made his reappearance in the heavens. Captain Gamblin, unhappily, did not long enjoy the sight of it. His health began to fail, and he was unable to make his customary observations. Under these depressing circumstances, the mate, finding the crew to become weaker day by day, prudently resolved to take in two reefs of the topsails, from the fear that all hands would be ineffective, if the vessel should get out to sea, and a gale come on. Only fifteen men were found able to go aloft on this duty, which was performed, according to an observation made by the mate, in latitude 69° 1', the drift still continuing southward. Four of the men died between the 19th of the month and the 1st of February; and two days after, the heaviest stroke of all befell the Dee, in the death of her beloved commander. Captain Gamblin's body was placed in a coffin to be carried home, at the desire of his friend Captain Taylor of the Grenville Bay; the other bodies were laid beneath the polar ice. To quote a solemn and expressive line of a humorous ballad,

" The iceberg is the monument that lies upon their graves."

Though the whalers were at this time three or four degrees farther south than at first, the frost was even more severe than ever. Every liquid was frozen; and while the snow was being melted to cook the victuals, the icicles were hanging on the water-cask, at the distance of six feet from the fire. The beds were covered with solid ice—the pillows frozen in every part but where the head lay, the very hairs of which were in some cases stiff with cold—and vermin of a more rapacious kind began to swarm among the blankets; creatures that ate their way through the skin, and fed on the raw flesh. And the men all the while bowed down with mortal sickness, and incapable of defending or cleaning themselves! So scarce was fuel, besides, that it could only be used for the melting of ice and cooking of victuals. Can we wonder that ere the 12th of February, six others of the crew sank under their distresses!

On the 13th, a good deal of water was seen not far off, but the bay ice was still strong. The latitude, according to an observation on this day, was 67° 32', and on the 16th it was 63° 33', showing the Dee to be moving rapidly to the south. The other vessels were advancing more slowly, the Advice being at this time not less than twenty miles farther north than the Dee. Between the 23d and 27th, six of the survivors of the latter vessel died, and by the 7th of March, other five had followed their departed mates. So many deaths as these enabled the remainder to enjoy full allowance of provisions. Six hands only were able at this time to do duty, and the ship was in great danger of a fatal squeeze from the state of the ice, which was loose, and rapidly breaking up. It was still so entire, however, as to permit the mate of the Dee to go over to the Grenville Bay, at this time not far off, and ask if Captain Taylor could render any assistance should the Dee get out into the open sea. Twenty of his men being on the sick list, Captain Taylor could promise no help. The Norfolk and Advice were about seven miles distant from the Dee on the 9th, and on the 11th, the whaler of Dundee was seen moving with her sails set, into the open sea. Between the 11th and 15th, three more of the Dee's crew died, and they were the last that were buried below the ice, which was now broken up in all directions. On the 16th, after being locked up for five months and eight days, the Dee entered into open water.

Great was the joy of the unhappy mariners, on this occasion, but, alas! many of those yet alive were destined never to see their native shores. Fortunately, light and favourable breezes attended, in general, the passage of the ship homewards, otherwise not one man of the Dee's crew could ever have reached his home. The scurvy raged so fearfully on board, that between the 16th of March and the 22d of April, twenty more of the men had fallen victims to it. A ship was seen on the 20th, but it does not seem to have perceived the signals of distress that were hoisted by the whaler. On the 25th, a fishing-boat was hailed, and it was found that the Dee was then off the Butt of Lewis. The fishermen in the boat cruelly refused to give any assistance, suspecting a case of plague, it is supposed. The barque Washington of Dundee, Barnett master, bound for New York, bore down upon the miserable whaler on the evening of the same day, and inquired if any assistance was wanted. On being informed of the state of matters, and that only three hands of the Dee were able to go aloft, Mr Barnett instantly sent four men on board, and followed in person, carrying with him wine, porter, and other provisions. He then took the Dee in tow, and enabled her to come to anchor, on the 27th of April, in the harbour of Stromness. Every attention was here paid to the survivors of the crew, and on the 5th of May, the owners having sent effective hands, the Dee was again put to sea and carried into the harbour of Aberdeen, after an absence of thirteen months and three days. A heart-rending scene took place on the quay, which was crowded with the relatives of the deceased seamen—with weeping widows, children, and parents. Forty-six men had died on board the Dee, nine of whom belonged to the Thomas of Dundee. Fourteen men only survived of the Dee's own complement.

Thus ended this unhappy voyage. In the Narrative from which the preceding account is condensed, and which has been drawn up from the notes of one of the survivors, David Gibb, and published at Aberdeen for his benefit, we find some judicious remarks on the propriety of storing whaling vessels, on all occasions, with a whole year's provisions and fuel, and also with a full medicine chest. Individual seamen are even recommended to provide themselves amply with coffee and sugar at their own expense. It is morally, and ought to be legally, incumbent upon all owners to attend to these directions, the product of dearly bought experience.

The companions of the Dee in adversity—the Norfolk, the Grenville Bay, and the Advice—all reached their respective places of outfit, in safety, as far as the vessels were concerned. The sufferings of the Advice, like those of the Dee, were terrible, and the loss of lives great. In the other two ships, much misery also had been endured. None of the distressed vessels, we believe, had the good fortune to fall in with the ships which their sympathising country sent to the northern seas for their relief.

ADVENTURE IN A VOYAGE TO THE LEVANT.

ONE evening lately, when at a small social party, we had the pleasure of sitting beside an old acquaintance, a Mr Kerr, one who had some time before returned from a foreign country, where for many years he had pursued a mercantile profession with advantage. In the course of our conversation, he alluded to a particular adventure he had once met in a voyage to the Levant, but immediately after seemed to shrink from the subject, as if the recollection of it were too painful to be endured. On my pressing the point, he at length, but with great reluctance, stated the following particulars:—*

"On my return, some years ago," said Kerr, "from the eastern coasts of the Mediterranean, which I had visited partly from curiosity, and partly with the view of furthering the mercantile pursuits in which I had engaged, I was induced, by what I had seen and learned, to freight a small vessel at Liverpool, with goods of various kinds, which I proposed to carry either to Alexandria or Beiroot. The vessel selected for this purpose was an Italian sloop, which seemed to me to be thrown in my way at the time by a piece of great good fortune. It had brought over a cargo from Italy, and the master

* As stories like the above are often only said to be true, we think it necessary to take this additional means of assuring the reader that the "Adventure in a Voyage to the Levant" is an incident which really occurred.

and crew, eight in number, and all natives of that country, were waiting in the Mersey, after discharging their freight, for any chance that might occur of returning to the Mediterranean with a fresh lading. This was an opportunity of the very kind I had wished, and an arrangement was speedily made with the Italian master, who engaged to convey my cargo to the first mentioned port on very reasonable terms. This matter settled, and the weather being favourable, I lost no time in making all the necessary preparations, and was soon enabled to set sail for the East, accompanied by my younger brother, the only other person on board besides the Italians and myself.

For a time, our voyage was a pleasant one. But before we entered the Straits of Gibraltar, the wind changed, and with it came changes, also, of another and more alarming kind. The master of the sloop, who was a middle-aged man, of sallow complexion, though with features not otherwise unpleasing, suddenly dropt the obsequiousness of his tone and manner, and appeared to shun all intercourse with my brother and myself. As the weather became more and more squally on our entering the Mediterranean, the man's behaviour became more and more distant and repulsive, and the expression of his eye at times was such as to excite the most unpleasant sensations in the mind of the two persons to whom it was directed, and who felt themselves wholly in his power. At length the thoughts brooding in the master's mind found vent in words. One day, as I stood on deck, the ship chanced to give a heavy lurch, and the Italian cried out, 'I am ruined, and that accursed fellow is the cause of it!' At the same moment he pointed to me, and cast on me a look full of hate and menace, which was reflected from the countenances of more than one of the crew. Similar expressions fell in mutterings from his lips day after day, until I became seriously alarmed, and for the first time consulted with my brother, to whom I had previously been unwilling to communicate my awakening fears. He had observed all that had passed, however, as closely and clearly as myself. Both of us were inclined, at first, to think that the fears of the master and the crew regarding the weather—for the Italians are timorous sailors—had only temporarily drowned their better feelings, and their reason also, seeing that the storm came not at our bidding. This explanation of their conduct proved but a pleasing illusion. The weather *improved*, but this circumstance was far from producing any favourable alteration in the deportment of the master and the crew. Their looks became more and more lowering; and, finally, open threats of *murder*, in daylight, and in hearing of almost every man on board, were vented against us by the master of the sloop!

My brother and myself had long been watchful and guarded in our movements, but this menace brought on a crisis. It was now but too plain that our destruction had been early meditated by the Italian captain, and that he had been hitherto merely lashing himself, as it were, into the proper pitch of fury, and gradually preparing the minds of his men for the entertainment and execution of the diabolical purpose. How dreadful was the condition in which we now found ourselves! In the centre of a vast sea—in which a thousand bodies might be buried and hid for ever from the eye of day—cribbed up in a small vessel in the midst of wretches ready and willing to destroy us—these enemies eight in number, while we were but two, and one of these two, a youth of eighteen—the feelings of persons in such a situation can be but faintly conceived by those who have never confronted danger in so terrible a form. Though feeling, however, the full horror of our position, we did not permit ourselves to be overcome by despair. The cabin appropriated to us fortunately contained our own stores of provision; and in this place, after the master's murderous threat, we shut ourselves up, barricading the door with all the heavy articles of furniture contained in the room. This proceeding was, as it were, a declaration of open war; it was an avowal of our knowledge of the purposes entertained against us; but it was the only step that could render us even for a moment secure.

The energies, bodily and mental, of human beings, frequently rise and become commensurate with the demands which occasion makes upon them. So I felt it to be with myself when I first laid down my head upon my pillow under the circumstances described. Above me, I heard the tread of assassins, whose thirst for my blood would not permit them to rest; beside me lay a beloved brother, entrusted to my charge by a doating mother far away; a sense of fearful danger and a feeling of deep anxiety were kept graven on my mind from these two present causes, independently of all considerations of individual peril to myself, and yet I did not feel sickened or depressed at the prospect before me. On the contrary, I felt a buoyancy, an energetic vigour, both of mind and body, which can only be ascribed to the exciting nature of the circumstances in which we were placed. As I painted to myself the possibility of a death-grapple—a struggle for the lives of my brother and myself—with the men by whom we were surrounded, I felt my muscles become as hard in every limb as a cable rope, and was conscious of possessing such capabilities of exertion, as would render my death no easy matter for even eight foes to accomplish.

This excited spirit did not forsake me. In the afternoon of the day following that on which we shut ourselves up, my brother and I found it impossible to endure any longer the close confinement of the cabin, without enjoying a mouthful of the fresh air; and after a consultation, the second that we had held that day, we came to the resolution of going together upon deck. At the same time, determined to sell our lives as dearly as possible, we armed ourselves, before leaving the cabin, with two large carving-knives with which the room was fortunately provided, and also took with us every other defensive weapon which we possessed. Thus equipped, we stepped upon the deck, locking the cabin door behind us. Glaring eyes, like those of hungry tigers, were fixed on us by the master and the crew, but the fire of watchful determination lit up the glances that were returned for theirs, and the villains quailed at the thought of attacking two resolute men, or, more probably, they calculated upon having a future opportunity of taking us off our guard. We were allowed, at least, to return to our cabin unmolested. But upon this we could build no hope of bettering our position. No man had spoken to us; no one had bid us good-morrow; every countenance was sullen, dark, and lowering.

For many consecutive days a similar scene was repeated. Armed in the manner described, we went once every twenty-four hours upon deck, and barricaded ourselves at every other time within our cabin. During each of these visits to the open air, every motion made by us was performed with such caution as became those whose movements were watched by demons, ready to spring upon their victims on the slightest show of incaution. But although it seems impossible that they could have been unsuccessful in a combined attack, their hearts uniformly failed them; for they saw well that some of them must have fallen—that we would not *die alone!*

Matters were in this situation—a situation still perilous and terrible, though we were growing accustomed to it—when, by my calculation of time, it seemed to me that we should be approaching the eastern Mediterranean coasts, as our course had not been changed, as far as I could observe. An alarming confirmation of this conjecture was presented to me one night as I sat alone in the cabin, my brother having laid himself down to sleep. The night was calm, and all was silent as my own brooding and voiceless thoughts, excepting the tramp—that often heard, that perpetual tramp—of two men walking upon the deck. These were the master and his mate — worthy and inseparable associates! Either they spoke louder, or the evening was stiller, than usual; for I distinctly heard the murmur of their voices, which, in the like situation, I had frequently endeavoured to catch in vain. I placed myself in the most favourable position for hearing, but my ear could gather sound only, not sense. At last, however, the voices increased in loudness—a violent stamp was made upon the cabin roof—and I heard the master's voice exclaim, with a curse which I shall not repeat, and in tones which showed that passion had for the moment got the better of prudence, ' It *must* be done to-morrow, Antoine! Cowards! to think that we should have shrunk so long from two men! But to-morrow they *must* die, or we lose our chance. We are close on shore, and will be boarded by some one immediately!' The mate appeared to have reminded him of his imprudence in making this loud exclamation, as they recommenced their walk, and their conversation sank to the same murmuring tone as before.

On that momentous night I closed not my eyes. The ruminations that kept me awake were of a mixed character. The sentence which I had overheard, although in one sense a death-knell, was in another a signal of hope. We were approaching the neighbourhood of human beings who were not our enemies—of those who might rescue us from the fangs of the murderous harpies in whose clutches we were. But, alas! could we repel the attack, could we survive the death-struggle, which was impending? To be ready for whatever might happen, I packed up all our most valuable articles, partly in a small box, and partly about my person. I resolved also not to acquaint my brother with the words of the master, but to go upon deck by myself on the following day, and bear the brunt of the anticipated assault alone. That I should go on deck, I was determined, as *there* only could the means of emancipation be found.

But my brother had not been asleep; he had heard the words of the master as distinctly as myself, and he insisted in the morning upon going with me upon deck, and sharing my peril, whatever it might be. Again, at this critical moment, did I feel in its full force all that tension of mind and body, of nerve and muscle, of which I have spoken. As I stepped on deck, I felt that the scowl which was cast upon me by the master, was returned by a glare of as tiger-like a character as his own. My glance rolled keenly from side to side, as I observed some more suspicious movements than usual on the part of the master and mate, and I prepared to buckler my dear brother's body with my own, and die —if I was to die—like a brave man! The fatal moment—the collision—was evidently drawing nigh, and I had again and again—silently but fervently—commended my soul to my Maker, when suddenly—'A ship! a ship in the offing!' was the cry from one of the crew. The master and the rest all ran to the farther end of the sloop, and gazed towards the vessel. I also would fain have gone and made signals to it, but dared not move from the spot. Things remained in this position for some minutes, the crew being still busy with the ship in the distance, when my brother touched me on the arm, and whispered hurriedly, 'A boat! a boat close under us!' It was so. A small boat, with four men in it, had come near to us unobserved. I made eager signs for it to lie to, and at the same time motioned my brother to bring the box from the cabin. He did so, noiselessly; in one moment it was in the boat, and in another we had sprung into it also, with all the energy of desperation. 'Row! row! for our lives and for your own; and for *this*,' was my earnest whisper to the boatmen, showing a purse, well filled with gold. The men seemed at once to comprehend that it was a case of peril, and pulled swiftly in the direction in which I pointed, which was, the reader may be assured, the opposite one to that in which the Italians still gazed. All this was the work of a moment, for it was work done by men whose faculties for exertion were indescribably aroused. When the crew of the sloop did observe our departure, we had made a considerable way from them, and all that they could do in their impotent rage and vexation was to send an unoffending shot or two after us. They did not attempt to follow. It may be, that, on consideration, they congratulated themselves on the possession of the cargo, which must have been the main object of their desires, and trusted never to see us again.

The first thought, it may be supposed, of my brother

and myself, on finding ourselves fairly free of the Italian sloop, was one of gratitude to heaven for our deliverance from that awful bondage. Our rescuers proved to be fishermen of the Delta, dwelling near the mouth of the Western Nile. Once safely ashore, and the personal jeopardy of my brother and myself ended, my mind—such is human nature—reverted to my property, and I resolved not to let the treacherous Italians off without making some attempt to reclaim what was my own. Calculating, from the point at which I was landed, that they would most probably run in for the port of Alexandria, I hired a boat to carry us across the Bay of Aboukir, and through Lake Mareotis to that city. My conjecture was correct; the Italian sloop was in the harbour. The authorities were applied to, and so strong were my proofs of a right to the cargo, that the greater part of it was yielded up to me; but a due consideration of the scanty chances of justice there, and a deficiency of evidence, made me depart from my original purpose of charging the wretches with their perfidious intent to murder. I was even obliged to enter into intercourse and compromise with the villanous master, before my goods could be unshipped and disposed of. My brother and I afterwards pursued our course by another vessel to Beiroot, where we made an advantageous sale of our cargo. It is only," Mr Kerr added, " because you have in a manner forced me to tell this story, that I have been induced to go through its details, for nothing can be more positively painful to me than to enter upon it. For months after my escape, I could not sleep soundly. For two years I could not allude to the incidents without losing a night's rest in consequence; and, even now, the mention of the circumstances puts me into a state of nervous agitation of a very distressing kind. May you never, my dear friend, pass twenty-two days in the way I spent them on my second voyage to the Levant!"

AN ADVENTURE AT SEA.

A NUMBER of years ago, said Captain M——, I was bound, in a fine stout ship of about four hundred tons burden, from the port of P—— to Liverpool. The ship had a valuable cargo on board, and about ninety thousand dollars in specie. I had been prevented, by other urgent business, from giving much of my attention to the vessel while loading and equipping for the voyage, but was very particular in my directions to the chief mate (in whom I had great confidence, he having sailed with me some years) to avoid entering, if possible, any but native American seamen. When we were about to sail, he informed me that he had not been able to comply with my directions entirely in this particular, but had shipped two foreigners as seamen, one a native of Guernsey, and the other a Frenchman from Brittany. I was pleased, however, with the appearance of the crew generally, and particularly with the foreigners. They were both stout and able-bodied men, and were particularly alert and attentive to orders.

The passage commenced auspiciously, and promised to be a speedy one, as we took a fine steady westerly wind soon after we lost soundings. To my great sorrow and uneasiness, I soon discovered in the foreigners a change of conduct for the worse. They became insolent to the mates, and appeared to be frequently under the excitement of liquor, and had evidently acquired an undue influence with the rest of the men. Their intemperance soon became intolerable; and as it was evident that they had brought liquor on board with them, I determined upon searching the forecastle, and depriving them of it. An order to this effect was given to the mates, and they were directed to go about its execution mildly but firmly, taking no arms with them as they seemed inclined to do, but to give every chest, berth, and locker in the forecastle, a thorough examination, and bring aft to the cabin any spirits they might find.

It was not without much anxiety that I sent them

forward upon this duty. I remained upon the quarter-deck myself, ready to go to their aid, should it be necessary. In a few moments, a loud and angry dispute was succeeded by a sharp scuffle around the forecastle companion-way. The steward, at my call, handed my loaded pistols from the cabin, and with them I hastened forward. The Frenchman had grappled the second mate, who was a mere lad, by the throat, thrown him across the heel of the bowsprit, and was apparently determined to strangle him to death. The chief mate was calling for assistance from below, where he was struggling with the Guernsey man. The rest of the crew were indifferent spectators, but rather encouraging the foreigners than otherwise. I presented a pistol at the head of the Frenchman, and ordered him to release the second mate, which he instantly did. I then ordered him into the foretop, and the others, who were near, into the maintop, none to come down under pain of death, until ordered. The steward had by this time brought another pair of pistols, with which I armed the second mate, directing him to remain on deck; and went below into the forecastle myself. I found that the chief mate had been slightly wounded in two places by the knife of his antagonist, who, however, ceased to resist as I made my appearance, and we immediately secured him in irons. The search was now made, and a quantity of liquor found and taken to the cabin. The rest of the men were then called down from the tops, and the Frenchman was made the companion of his coadjutor's confinement. I then expostulated, at some length, with the others upon their improper and insubordinate conduct, and upon the readiness with which they had suffered themselves to be drawn into such courses by two rascally foreigners, and expressed hopes that I should have no reason for further complaint during the rest of the voyage. This remonstrance I thought had effect, as they appeared contrite, and promised amendment. They were then dismissed, and order was restored.

The next day the foreigners strongly solicited pardon,

with the most solemn promises of future good conduct; and as the rest of the crew joined in their request, I ordered that their irons should be taken off. For several days the duties of the ship were performed to my entire satisfaction; but I could discover in the countenances of the foreigners expressions of deep and rancorous animosity to the chief mate, who was a prompt, energetic seaman, requiring from the sailors, at all times, a ready and implicit obedience to his orders.

A week perhaps had passed over in this way, when one night, in the mid watch, all hands were called to shorten sail. Ordinarily upon occasions of this kind, the duty was conducted by the mate, but I now went upon deck myself and gave orders, sending him upon the forecastle. The night was dark and squally, but the sea was not high, and the ship was running off about nine knots, with the wind upon the starboard quarter. The weather being very unpromising, the second reef was taken in the fore and main topsails, the mizen handed, and the fore and mizen top-gallant yards sent down. This done, one watch was permitted to go below, and I prepared to betake myself to my berth again, directing the mate, to whom I wished to give some orders, should be sent to me. To my utter astonishment and consternation, word was brought me, after a short time, that he was nowhere to be found. I hastened upon deck, ordered all hands up again, and questioned every man in the ship upon the subject; but they, with one accord, declared that they had not seen the mate forward. Lanterns were then brought, and every accessible part of the vessel was unavailingly searched. I then, in the hearing of the whole crew, declared my belief that he must have fallen overboard by accident, again dismissed one watch below, and repaired to the cabin, in a state of mental agitation impossible to be described; for, notwithstanding the opinion which I had expressed to the contrary, I could not but entertain strong suspicions that the unfortunate man had met a violent death.

The second mate was a protegé of mine, and, as

I have before observed, was a very young man, of not much experience as a seaman. I therefore felt that, under critical circumstances, my main support had fallen from me. It is needless to add, that a deep sense of forlornness and insecurity was the result of these reflections.

My first step was to load and deposit in my state-room all the fire-arms on board, amounting to several muskets and four pairs of pistols. The steward was a faithful mulatto man, who had sailed with me several voyages. To him I communicated my suspicions, and directed him to be constantly on the alert, and should any further difficulty with the crew occur, to repair immediately to my state-room and arm himself. His usual berth was in the steerage, but I further directed that he should, on the following morning, clear out and occupy one in the cabin near my own. The second mate occupied a small state-room opening into the passage which led from the steerage to the cabin. I called him from the deck, gave him a pair of loaded pistols, with orders to keep them in his berth, and, during his night watches on deck, never to go forward of the main mast, but to continue as constantly as possible near the cabin companion-way, and call me upon the slightest occasion. After this, I lay down in my bed, ordering that I should be called at four o'clock for the morning watch. Only a few minutes had elapsed, when I heard three or four knocks under the counter of the ship, which is that part of the stern immediately under the cabin windows. In a minute or two they were distinctly repeated. I arose, opened the cabin window, and called. *The mate answered!* I gave him the end of a rope to assist him up, and never shall I forget the flood of gratitude which my delighted soul poured forth to that Being who had restored him to me *uninjured*. His story was soon told. He had gone forward upon being ordered by me, after the calling of all hands, and had barely reached the forecastle, when he was seized by the two foreigners, and before he could utter more than one cry, which was drowned in the roaring of the winds and waves, was thrown over the bow. He was a powerful man, and an excellent swimmer. The topsails of the ship were clewed down to reef, and her way, of course, considerably lessened; and in an instant he found the end of a rope, which was accidentally towing overboard, within his grasp, by which he dragged in the dead water, or eddy, that is always created under the stern of a vessel while sailing, particularly if she is full built and deeply laden, as was the case with this. By a desperate effort he caught one of the rudder chains, which was very low, and drew himself by it upon the step or jog of the rudder, where he had sufficient presence of mind to remain without calling out, until the light had ceased to shine through the cabin windows, when he concluded that the search for him was over. He then made the signal to me.

No being in the ship but myself was apprised of his safety; for the gale had increased, and completely drowned the sounds of the knocking, opening the window, &c., before they could reach the quarterdeck; and there was no one in the cabin but ourselves, the steward having retired to his berth in the steerage. It was at once resolved that the second mate only should be informed of his existence. He immediately betook himself to a large vacant state-room, and for the remainder of the passage all his wants were attended to by me. Even the steward was allowed to enter the cabin as rarely as possible.

Nothing of note occurred during the remainder of the voyage, which was prosperous. It seemed that the foreigners had only been actuated by *revenge* in the violence they had committed, for nothing further was attempted by them. In due season we took a pilot in the Channel, and in a day or two entered the port of Liverpool. As soon as the proper arrangements were made, we commenced warping the ship into dock, and while engaged in this operation, *the mate appeared on deck, went forward, and attended to his duties as usual!* A scene occurred which is beyond description: every feature of it is as vivid in my recollection as though it had occurred but yesterday, and will be to my latest breath. The warp dropped from the paralysed hands of the horror-stricken sailors, and had it not been taken up by some boatmen on board, I should have been compelled to anchor again, and procure assistance from the shore. Not a word was uttered; but the two guilty wretches staggered to the mainmast, where they remained petrified with horror, until the officer who had been sent for, approached to take them into custody. They then seemed in a measure to be recalled to a sense of their appalling predicament, and uttered the most piercing expressions of lamentation and despair. They were soon tried, and upon the testimony of the mate, capitally convicted and executed.*

SCENE WITH A PIRATE.

In the month of July 1813, I was on my way from New York to the island of Curaçoa, on board the American ship Patrick Henry, commanded by Captain Tuttle. We had had a fine passage, and were looking forward to the end of our voyage in about a week. I was the only passenger, and of course was thrown in a great measure on my own resources for amusement, the chief of which was testing the powers of an admirable glass, of London manufacture, upon every vessel that showed itself above the horizon. Our captain was kind and civil, but there appeared a mystery about him that he did not like to be pried into, and our communication had in consequence been reserved.

In about latitude 20 degrees, and longitude 60 degrees 15 minutes, we were running along with a fine fresh breeze abeam, and all our weather studding-sails set. I was sitting alone in the cabin, ruminating upon the

* We quote the foregoing from an American publication, which does not mention the name of the author by whom the piece was composed.

changes of scene and society into which I had been forced so contrary to my inclinations, and wondering whether the happiness of a quiet and domestic life was ever to fall to my lot, when the captain came down and told me that, as I was so fond of using my glass, there was a vessel just appearing on the horizon to windward, and that I might go and see what she was, for he could not make her out at all. I went on deck, and mounted into the maintop, and began my scrutiny. "Well, what is she?" asked the captain from the deck. "I can hardly make her out, but I think she is a schooner." "Ay—what's her course?" "South-west by south, I think; about the same as ourselves." I remained in the top for a few minutes, and continued looking at the stranger. "She seems fonder of the sea than I am," I continued, "for she might have her topsails and top-gallants, and studding-sails to boot, all set, instead of slipping along under her lower sails." The captain made no answer, but was looking hard at her with his eye. I now perceived through my glass a white speck above her foresail, flap, flapping against the mast. "Well, she must have heard me, for there goes her fore-topsail." The captain now went to the companion for his glass, and after looking attentively at her for a short time—"What's that?" he asked; "is that her square-sail she's setting? I can't very well see from the deck." I looked again: "Yes, 'tis her square-sail; as I'm alive, she's changed her course, and is bearing down upon us." But by this time the captain had mounted the rigging, and was standing beside me; he was eyeing the distant vessel keenly. After having apparently satisfied himself, he asked me to go with him to the cabin, as he wished to talk with me alone. We descended to the deck, and I followed him to the cabin. He motioned me to take a seat, and after carefully shutting the door, "I rather expect," said he, "that fellow's a pirate." "Pirate?" I asked, in alarm. "Yes, I say pirate, and I'll tell you why. In the first place, you see, he'd no business to be sneaking along in that do-little sort of a way, as when we first saw him;

who ever, that had any honest business to do, would allow such a fine breeze to go by without showing more canvass than a powder-monkey's old breeches to catch it? Next, you see, what the mischief has he to do with us, that, as soon as he clapped eyes on us, he must alter his course, and be so anxious to get out his square-sail? Again, he looks just like one of those imps of mischief, with his low black hull and tall raking masts. But it's no use talking; I tell you he's a pirate, and that's as true as my name's Isaac Tuttle. And now the only thing is, what shall we do? The Patrick Henry ain't a Baltimore clipper, and that 'ere devil will walk up to us like nothin'. But I'll tell you what strikes me:— If we let them devils aboard, it's most likely we'll all walk the plank; so we'd better try to keep 'em out. We h'aint got but an old rusty carronade and two six-pounders, and I don't believe there's a ball on board, we came off in such a hurry. Then, there's two muskets and an old regulation rifle down in my state-room; but they h'aint been fired I don't know when, and I'd as lief stand afore 'em as behind 'em. But our ship's as handsome a looking craft as you'll see; and couldn't we look wicked-like now, and try to frighten that cut-throat-looking rascal?"

I confess I was at first startled at the captain's opinion of the strange sail, and his reasoning left me hardly a hope that his judgment was not correct; but his cool and collected manner impressed me with confidence in his management, and I told him he knew best what we should do, and I would second him as I best could. He walked up and down the cabin twice; then rubbing his hands together as if pleased with his own idea—" I have it!" he cried; "I'll just go on deck to put things in order, and in the mean time you'd better amuse yourself looking out your pistols, if you have any; for if he wont be content with a look at us, we'll have to fight."

I hurriedly took my fowling-piece and pistols from their cases, for I fortunately had both; and though I somehow refused to allow myself to believe there would be any occasion for their use, yet I loaded them all with ball, and in each of the pistols put a brace; this done, I went on deck, where I found the captain surrounded by his crew, telling them his suspicions, and his plan of action. " But," said he, " maybe we'll have to fight; if them devils have a mind to try us, they'll send a boat on board, and I want to know if you'll help me to keep 'em off. You see it's most likely they'll make you walk the plank, whether you fight or not, if they get on board; and I calculate, if you do just as I tell you, we'll frighten 'em." There was a hearty " Ay, ay, sir," to this short and pithy harangue. " Thankee, thankee, boys," said the captain; " now we'll not show another stitch of canvass, but seem to take no more notice of that fellow than if we didn't see him; and if he does try to come aboard, then we'll show 'em what we can do."

Our captain was about fifty years old, rather short and stout, but muscular; his face was bronzed with time and tempest, and his locks, which had once been black, were grizzled by the same causes. He was an old sailor and a staunch republican; and as some of his men told tales of fight in which their captain had borne a part, I presumed he had served when a young man in the navies of the states.

The crew were busy, in obedience to his orders, cutting up a spare foretop-gallant-mast into logs of about four feet long; these were immediately painted black, with a round spot in the centre of one end, so as to bear a tolerable resemblance to pieces of cannon, and, with two old six-pounders, were placed, one at each port, on our deck, five on a side; but the ports were to be kept closed until the captain gave the order to open them, when they were to be raised as quickly as possible, and the logs thrust out about a foot. A platform was then made on the top of the long-boat, which was fixed between the fore and main masts, and the carronade, or fourteen-pounder, was hoisted up. These things being arranged, the captain went below, and the crew mustered in knots, to wonder and talk of what was to be done.

In the mean time, we had been standing on our course, and had not shifted or hoisted a single sail, but were as if perfectly regardless of the schooner. Not so with her, however; for besides a large squaresail and square-topsail on the fore-mast, she had run out small fore-topmast studding-sails, and onward she came right before a pretty smart breeze, yawing from side to side, at one moment sinking stern foremost into the trough of the sea, as an enormous wave rolled out from under her, and at the next forced headlong onwards by its successor, while a broad white sheet of foam spread out around her, giving beautiful relief to the jet-black colour of her hull, testifying how rapidly she was going through the water. I could not help thinking of the captain's expression, for she certainly did " walk up to us like nothin'," and as there appeared to be not much time to lose, I went down to the cabin to assume my weapons. The captain was there arranging some papers, and a bottle was before him into which he had put a letter. " May be," said he, " something 'ill happen to me; for if them 'ere bloody devils won't be cheated, I will be the first to suffer; and natural enough too, for all the mischief they'll suffer will be by my orders, just because I didn't like to be overhauled like an old tarpaulin by every rascal that chooses to say heave to, in the high seas. But never mind; only, should you escape, just drop the bottle and letter overboard, if you think you can't deliver it yourself."

Now, I had never seriously considered the probability that I might also be killed in an approaching melée, for I thought that the captain intended to throw open his ports and show his sham guns, and that, of course, the schooner would take fright. But when he began to talk about death in such a serious strain, I began to feel very uncomfortable; and not being naturally a warrior, I wished myself any where else than on board the Patrick Henry. There I was, however, without a chance of escape; and I suggested to the captain that it would be as well for me to put a letter into the bottle also, in case of any accident to both of us, which was agreed to; and we arranged that if either survived and had the opportunity, the letter of the unfortunate should be safely forwarded to its destination. After this little piece of preparation, the captain took me by the hand. "'Tis well," said he; "are you willing to share with me the post of danger? Do not suppose I am unaccustomed to the perils of a sea-fight: no, young man; I've supported the glory of the thirteen stripes in many a gallant action, and have witnessed the death of those honoured and esteemed as the sons of liberty. Yet they were fighting for their country, and it was their duty to hold their lives cheap; but you are a passenger, and should be under my protection—yet I ask you to share my danger. I wish some one to stand by me on the platform, and help me to manage the swivel. Hands are scarce, and I don't know where else to place you." The hardy fellow's eyes glistened as he made the proposal, to which I of course instantly agreed. "Thankee, thankee," he replied, and relapsed into his former character. 'Twas strange; he had always appeared on board his vessel as a common Yankee captain, with little to say, and with a rough uncouth manner but little removed from his men. Yet he at once, though evidently inadvertently, assumed the air and manner of a polished gentleman; and it certainly struck me that the latter character appeared more natural to him than the former. There was evidently a mystery about him, and I determined to find it out when more opportune circumstances should occur.

We went on deck, and the men were still hanging about waiting for the orders of their captain to make them start. These were soon given. The cooper and the carpenter were ordered to bring up all the hatchets, and other offensive and defensive weapons, and with the muskets and rifle they were distributed among the crew, who received their orders to use them in repelling any attempt to board.

The schooner had now come down within half a mile of us, when she suddenly took down her squaresail, and hauled her wind, to have a look at us. I daresay she did not know what to make of our seeming indifference. Presently a cloud of smoke burst from her side, and a ball came skipping over the water, and passed astern of us. "I thought so," said the captain; "now, lads, show her our stripes." A ball of bunting flew up to the end of our mizen peak, rested an instant, and fluttered out into the American ensign. The smoke drifted away from the schooner, and she ran up at her gaff the ensign of the Columbian republic. "That's 'ternally the way with them blackguards; they're always making a fool of some republic." Scarcely were the words out of his mouth, when another column of smoke burst from the schooner, and another ball came skip, skipping along towards us, but, catching a swell, it plunged in, and we saw no more of it. "That fellow now, I take it, is a good shot, so we'll not wait for another. Clue up the mainsail, boys; haul aft the weather mainbraces; clue up the foresail; luff her, man, luff her a little more—steady," burst from our captain's mouth: the orders were obeyed with the quickness of a well-disciplined crew, and our ship was hove to. "Now, my lads, take your stations, four to each port on the weather side, but do nothin' till I tell ye." The men took their stations, as directed, round each log on the weather side, and I followed the captain to the platform where our carronade was mounted. It was loaded to the muzzle with bits of iron, musket-balls, lumps of lead, and various other missiles, for the captain had conjectured truly—there were no balls on board. The schooner hove to, and a boat was lowered, and crowded with men. It approached rapidly, pulled by eight rowers. The muzzle of our carronade was depressed as much as possible, and made to bear on the water about fifty yards from the ship. The captain stood with his speaking-trumpet in one hand, and a handspike, with which he shifted the position of the gun as required, in the other. The schooner's boat approached, and was pulling rapidly to get alongside. "Now, sir, keep steady, and obey my orders coolly," said the captain, in an under tone. "Boy, fetch the iron that's heating in the galley—run." The boy ran, and returned with the iron rod heated at one end, which was handed to me. " When I tell you to fire, fire, as you value your life and those on board." The captain now put his speaking-trumpet to his mouth, and hailed the boat, which was within a hundred yards of us. " Stop—no nearer, or I'll blow you all out of the water—keep off, keep off, or, I say, I'll——" At that instant the man at the bows of the boat, who appeared to take the command, gave an order, and a volley from several muskets was fired at us. I heard the balls hit about me, and turned to look for the captain to receive my order to fire. He was on one knee behind the cannon, and holding it by the breech. " Why, captain! what's the matter?—are you hit?" He rallied. " Nothing— they're coming." He gave another hoist to the gun, cast his eye hurriedly along its barrel —" *Fire*, and be quick!" I needed not a second bidding, for the boat was close alongside. The smoke burst from the touch-hole with a hiss, and for an instant I thought the gun had missed fire, but in the next it exploded with a tremendous report, that deafened me. " Throw open your ports, boys, and show them your teeth," roared the captain through his trumpet, and his voice sounded hideously unnatural. In an instant every port was up, and our guns protruded their muzzles. I had fancied that I heard a crash, followed by wild screams, immediately upon the discharge of the cannon; but the report had deafened me; and the smoke, which was driven back in my face, had so shrouded me, that I could not see; the unearthly shout of the captain had also for the moment driven the idea from my mind, and I now grasped my gun to repel boarders. But my hearing had not deceived me; for, as the smoke was borne away to leeward, the whole scene of destruction burst upon my sight. The cannon had been most truly pointed, and its contents had shivered the hapless boat, killing or wounding almost every person in her. The longest lifetime will hardly efface that scene from my mind. The stern of the boat had been carried completely away, and it was sinking by the weight of the human beings that clung to it. As it gradually disappeared, the miserable wretches straggled forward to the bows, and with horrid screams and imprecations battled for a moment for what little support it might yield. The dead and the dying were floating and splashing around them, while a deep crimson tinge marked how fatal had been that discharge. Ropes were thrown over, and every thing done to save those that were not destroyed by the cannon-shot, but only three out of the boat's crew of twenty-four were saved; the greater part went down with the boat to which they clung.

The whole scene of destruction did not last ten minutes, and all was again quiet. The bodies of those who had been shot did not sink, but were driven by the wind and sea against the side of the ship. From some the blood was gently oozing, and floating around them; others, stiff in the convulsion in which they had died, were grinning or frowning with horrible expression. One body, strong and muscular, with neat white trousers, and a leathern girdle in which were stuck two pistols, floated by, but the face was gone; some merciless ball had so disfigured him, that all trace of human expression was destroyed. He was the pirate captain.

But where was the schooner? She lay for a few minutes after the destruction of her boat; and whether alarmed at our appearance, or horrified at the loss of so many of her men, I know not, but she slipped her foresail, and stood away as close to the wind as possible. We saw no more of her.

The excitement of the scene we had just passed through prevented our missing the captain; but so soon as the schooner bore away, all naturally expected his voice to give some order for getting again under way. But no order came. Where was he? The musket discharge from the boat, with the unearthly voice that conveyed the orders for the ports to be thrown open, flashed across my mind. I ran to the platform. The captain was there lying on his face beside the gun that he had pointed with such deadly effect. He still grasped the speaking-trumpet in his hand, and I shuddered as I beheld its mouth-piece covered with blood. "The captain's killed!" I cried, and stooped to raise him. "I believe I am," said he; "take me to the cabin." A dozen ready hands were stretched to receive him, and he was taken below, and carefully laid on a sofa. "Ay," he said, "I heard the crash; my ear knows too well the crash of shot against a plank to be mistaken, and my eye has pointed too many guns to miss its mark easily now. But, tell me, is any one else hurt?" "No, thank God," I said; "and I hope you are not so badly hit." "Bad enough. But cut open my waistcoat—'tis here." A mouthful of blood stopped his utterance, but he pointed to his right side. I wiped his mouth, and we cut off his waistcoat as gently as possible. There was no blood; but on removing his shirt, we discovered, about three inches on the right of the pit of the stomach, a discoloured spot, about the size of half-a-crown, darkening towards its centre, where there was a small wound. A musket ball had struck him, and from there being no outward bleeding, I feared the worst. We dressed the wound as well as circumstances would permit; but externally it was trifling—the fatal wound was within. The unfortunate sufferer motioned for all to leave him but me; and calling me to his side, "I feel," said he, "that I am dying; the letter—promise me that you will get it forwarded—'tis to my poor widow. Well, I've tempted this death often and escaped, and 'tis hard to be struck by a villain's hand. But God's will be done." I promised that I would personally deliver the letter, for that I intended returning to New York from Curaçoa. "Thank you truly," said the dying man; "you will then see my Helen and my child, and can tell them that their unfortunate husband and father died thinking of them. This ship and cargo are mine, and will belong to my family. Stranger, I was not always what I now seem. But I could not bear that the Yankee skipper should be known as he who once——" A sudden flow of blood prevented his finishing the sentence. I tried to relieve him by change of posture, but in vain; he muttered some incoherent sentences, by which his mind seemed to dwell upon former scenes of battle for the republic, and of undeserved treatment. He rallied for one instant, and, with a blessing for his family, and the name of Helen on his lips, he ceased to breathe.

The body of our unfortunate captain was next day committed to the waves, amidst the tears of us all. Our voyage was prosecuted to an end without further interruption. I did not forget the wishes of the dying man; how faithfully I fulfilled them, and how I have been rewarded, or how satisfactory to me was the previous history of the poor captain, need not be told. Suffice it to say, that I am settled in Elm Cottage, Bloemendaal, and am the happiest son-in-law, husband, and father, in the United States.

MOCHA DICK,

OR THE WHITE WHALE OF THE PACIFIC.

[Abridged from the Knickerbocker, or New York Monthly Magazine, where it appeared in May 1839. Mocha, from which the whale takes its name, is a small island off the coast of Chili, in latitude 38 degrees 28 minutes south. The story of the conquest of Mocha Dick is narrated by an intrepid American "whaler," on board a whale vessel in the Pacific; but before entering into the particulars of this triumph, the author gives a preliminary account of this famed monster of the deep.]

MOCHA DICK, who had come off victorious in a hundred fights with his pursuers, was an old bull whale, of prodigious size and strength. From the effect of age, or more probably from a freak of nature, as exhibited in the case of the Ethiopian albino, a singular consequence had resulted—*he was white as wool!* Instead of projecting his spout obliquely forward, and puffing with a short convulsive effort, accompanied by a snorting noise, as usual with his species, he flung the water from his nose in a lofty perpendicular expanded volume, at regular and somewhat distant intervals; its expulsion producing a continuous roar, like that of vapour struggling from the safety-valve of a powerful steam-engine. Viewed from a distance, the practised eye of the sailor only could decide, that the moving mass which constituted this enormous animal, was not a white cloud sailing along the horizon. On the spermaceti whale, barnacles are rarely discovered; but upon the head of this *lusus naturæ* they had clustered, until it became absolutely rugged with the shells. In short, regard him as you would, he was a most extraordinary fish; or, in the vernacular of Nantucket, " a genuine old sog" of the first water.

Opinions differ as to the time of his discovery. It is settled, however, that previous to the year 1810, he had been seen and attacked near the island of Mocha. Numerous boats are known to have been shattered by his immense flukes, or ground to pieces in the crush of his powerful jaws; and it is said that on one occasion he came off victorious from a conflict with the crews of three English whalers, striking fiercely at the last of the retreating boats, at the moment it was rising from the water, in its hoist up to the ship's davits. It must not be supposed, howbeit, that through all this desperate warfare our leviathan passed scathless. A back serried with irons, and from fifty to a hundred yards of line trailing in his wake, sufficiently attested, that though unconquered, he had not proved invulnerable. From the period of Dick's first appearance, his celebrity continued to increase, until his name seemed naturally to mingle with the salutations which whalemen were in the habit of exchanging in their encounters upon the broad Pacific; the customary interrogatories almost always closing with, "Any news from Mocha Dick?" Indeed, nearly every whaling captain who rounded Cape Horn, if he possessed any professional ambition, or valued himself on his skill in subduing the monarch of the seas, would lay his vessel along the coast, in the hope of having an opportunity to try the muscle of this doughty champion, who was never known to shun his assailants. It was remarked, nevertheless, that the old fellow seemed particularly careful as to the portion of his body which he exposed to the approach of the boat-steerer; generally presenting, by some well-timed manœuvre, his back to the harpooner, and dexterously evading every attempt to plant an iron under his fin, or a spade on his " small." Though naturally fierce, it was not customary with Dick, while unmolested, to betray a malicious disposition. On the contrary, he would sometimes pass quietly round a vessel, and occasionally swim lazily and harmlessly among the boats, when armed with full craft for the destruction of his race. But this forbearance gained him little credit; for if no other cause of accusation remained to them, his foes would swear they saw a lurking devilry in the long careless sweep of his flukes. Be this as it may, nothing is more certain than that all indifference vanished with the first prick of the harpoon; while cutting the line, and a hasty retreat to their vessel, were frequently the only means of escape from destruction left to his discomfited assaulters.

" I will not weary you," said the whaler, " with the uninteresting particulars of a voyage to Cape Horn. Our vessel, as capital a ship as ever left the little island of Nantucket, was finely manned and commanded, as well as thoroughly provided with every requisite for the peculiar service in which she was engaged. I may here observe, for the information of such among you as are not familiar with these things, that soon after a whale-ship from the United States is fairly at sea, the men are summoned aft; then boats' crews are selected by the captain and first mate, and a ship-keeper, at the same time, is usually chosen. The place to be filled by this individual is an important one, and the person designated should be a careful and sagacious man. His duty is, more particularly, to superintend the vessel while the boats are away in chase of fish; and at these times the cook and steward are perhaps his only crew. His station, on these occasions, is at the mast-head, except when he is wanted below to assist in working the ship. While aloft, he is to look out for whales, and also to keep a strict and tireless eye upon the absentees, in order to render them immediate assistance should emergency require it. Should the game rise to windward of their pursuers, and they be too distant to observe personal signs, he must run down the jib. If they rise to leeward, he should haul up the spanker; continuing the little black signal-flag at the mast so long as they remain on the surface. When the 'school' turn flukes, and go down, the flag is to be struck, and again displayed when they are seen to ascend. When circumstances occur which require the return of the captain on board, the colours are to hoisted at the mizen peak. A ship-keeper must further be sure that provisions are ready for the men on their return from the chase, and that drink be amply furnished, in the form of a bucket of 'switchel.'

I have already said that little of interest occurred, until after we had doubled Cape Horn. We were now standing in upon the coast of Chili, before a gentle breeze from the south, that bore us along almost imperceptibly. It was a quiet and beautiful evening, and the sea glanced and glistened in the level rays of the descending sun, with a surface of waving gold. The western sky was flooded with amber light, in the midst of which, like so many islands, floated immense clouds, of every conceivable brilliant dye; while far to the north-east, looming darkly against a paler heaven, rose the conical peak of Mocha. The men were busily employed in sharpening their harpoons, spades, and lances, for the expected fight. The look-out at the mast-head, with cheek on his shoulder, was dreaming of the 'dangers he had passed,' instead of keeping watch for those which were to come; while the captain paced the quarterdeck with long and hasty stride, scanning the ocean in every direction, with a keen, expectant eye. All at once he stopped, fixed his gaze intently for an instant on some object to leeward, that seemed to attract it, and then, in no very conciliating tone, hailed the mast-head: 'Both ports shut!' he exclaimed, looking aloft, and pointing backward, where a long white bushy spout was rising, about a mile off the larboard bow, against the glowing horizon. 'Both ports shut,' I say, 'you leaden-eyed lubber! Nice lazy son of a sea-cook *you* are, for a look-out! Come down, sir!'

'There she blows!—sperm whale—old sog, sir,' said the man, in a deprecatory tone, as he descended from his nest in the air. It was at once seen that the creature was companionless; but as a lone whale is generally an old bull, and of unusual size and ferocity, more than ordinary sport was anticipated, while unquestionably more than ordinary honour was to be won from its successful issue.

The second mate and I were ordered to make ready for pursuit; and now commenced a scene of emulation and excitement, of which the most vivid description would convey but an imperfect outline, unless you have been a spectator or an actor on a similar occasion. Line-tubs, water-kegs, and wafe-poles, were thrown hurriedly into the boats; the irons were placed in the racks, and the necessary evolutions of the ship gone through, with a quickness almost magical; and this, too, amidst what to a landsman would have seemed inextricable confusion, with perfect regularity and precision; the commands of the officers being all but forestalled by the enthusiastic eagerness of the men. In a short time we were as near the object of our chase as it was considered prudent to approach.

'Back the main-top-s'l!' shouted the captain. 'There she blows! there she blows! there she blows!' cried the look-out, who had taken the place of his sleepy shipmate, raising the pitch of his voice with each announcement, until it amounted to a downright yell. 'Right ahead, sir!—spout as long an 's thick as the mainyard!'

'Stand by to lower!' exclaimed the captain; 'all hands—cook, steward, cooper, every one of ye, stand by to lower!'

An instantaneous rush from all quarters of the vessel answered this appeal, and every man was at his station almost before the last word had passed the lips of the skipper.

'Lower away!' and in a moment the keels splashed in the water. 'Follow down the crews: jump in, my boys; ship the crotch; line your oars; now pull as if the d—l was in your wake!' were the successive orders as the men slipped down the ship's side, took their places in the boats, and began to give way.

The second mate had a little the advantage of me in starting. The stern of his boat grated against the bows of mine at the instant I grasped my steering-oar and gave the word to shove off. One sweep of my arm, and we sprang foaming in his track. Now came the tug of war. To become a first-rate oarsman, you must understand, requires a natural gift. My crew were not wanting in the proper qualification; every mother's son of them pulled as if he had been born with an oar in his hand; and as they stretched every sinew for the glory of darting the first iron, it did my heart good to see the boys spring. At every stroke the tough blades bent like willow wands, and quivered like tempered steel in the warm sunlight, as they sprang forward from the retreating wave. At the distance of half a mile, and directly before us, lay the object of our emulation and ambition, heaving his huge bulk in unwieldy gambols, as though totally unconscious of our approach.

'There he blows! An old bull, by Jupiter! Eighty barrels, boys, waiting to be towed alongside! Long and quick—shoot ahead! Now she feels it; waist-boat never could beat us; now she feels the touch! now she walks through it! Again—*now!*' Such were the broken exclamations and adjurations with which I cheered my rowers to their toil, as, with renewed vigour, I plied my long steering-oar. In another moment we were alongside our competitor. The shivering blades flashed forward and backward, like sparks of light. The waters boiled under our prow, and the trenched waves closed, hissing and whirling in our wake, as we swept, I might almost say were *lifted*, onward in our arrowy course.

We were coming down upon our fish, and could hear the roar of his spouting above the rush of the sea, when my boat began to take the lead.

'Now, my fine fellows,' I exclaimed in triumph, 'now we'll show them our stern—only spring! Stand ready, harpooner, but don't dart till I give the word.'

'Carry me on, and his name's *Dennis!*'* cried the boat-steerer, in a confident tone. We were perhaps a hundred feet in advance of the waist-boat, and within fifty of the whale, about an inch of whose hump only was to be seen above the water, when, heaving slowly into view a pair of flukes some eighteen feet in width, he went down. The men lay on their oars. 'There he blows again!' cried the tub-oarsman, as a lofty perpendicular spout sprang into the air, a few furlongs away on the starboard side. Presuming, from his previous movement, that the old fellow had been 'gallied' by other boats, and might probably be jealous of our purpose, I was about ordering the men to pull away as softly and silently as possible, when we received fearful intimation that he had no intention of baulking our inclination, or even yielding us the honour of the first attack. Lashing the sea with his enormous tail, until he threw about him a cloud of surf and spray, he came down, at full speed, 'jaws on,' with the determination, apparently, of doing battle in earnest. As he drew near, with his long curved back looming occasionally above the surface of the billows, we perceived that it was *white as the surf around him;* and the men stared aghast at each other, as they uttered, in a suppressed tone, the terrible name of MOCHA DICK.'

'Mocha Dick!' said I; 'this boat never sheers off from any thing that wears the shape of a whale. Pull easy; just give her way enough to steer.' As the creature approached, he somewhat abated his phrensied speed, and, at the distance of a cable's length, changed his course to a sharp angle with our own.

'Here he comes!' I exclaimed. 'Stand up, harpooner! Don't be hasty—don't be flurried. Hold your iron higher, firmer. Now!' I shouted, as I brought our bows within a boat's length of the immense mass

---

* A whale's name is " Dennis," when he spouts blood.

which was wallowing heavily by. '*Now—give it to him solid!*'

But the leviathan plunged on unharmed. The young harpooner, though ordinarily as fearless as a lion, had imbibed a sort of superstitious dread of Mocha Dick, from the exaggerated stories of that prodigy, which he had heard from his comrades. He regarded him, as he had heard him described in many a tough yarn during the middle watch, rather as some ferocious fiend of the deep, than a regular-built, legitimate whale. Judge, then, of his trepidation, on beholding a creature answering the wildest dreams of his fancy, and sufficiently formidable, without any superadded terrors, bearing down upon him with thrashing flukes and distended jaws! He stood erect, it cannot be denied. He planted his foot—he grasped the coil—he poised his weapon. But his knee shook, and his sinewy arm wavered. The shaft was hurled, but with unsteady aim. It just grazed the back of the monster, glanced off, and darted into the sea beyond. A second, still more abortive, fell short of the mark. The giant animal swept on for a few rods, and then, as if in contempt of our fruitless and childish attempt to injure him, flapped a storm of spray in our faces with his broad tail, and dashed far down into the depths of the ocean, leaving our little skiff among the waters where he sank, to spin and duck in the whirlpool.

Night being now at hand, the captain's signal was set for our return to the vessel, and we were soon assembled on her deck, discussing the mischances of the day, and speculating on the prospect of better luck on the morrow.

We were at breakfast next morning, when the watch at the foretop-gallant head sang out merrily, 'There she breaches!' In an instant every one was on his feet. 'Where away?' cried the skipper, rushing from the cabin, and upsetting in his course the steward, who was returning from the caboose with a replenished biggin of hot coffee. 'Not loud but deep' were the grumblings and groans of that functionary, as he rubbed his scalded shins, and danced about in agony; but had they been far louder, they would have been drowned in the tumult of vociferation which answered the announcement from the mast-head.

'Where away?' repeated the captain, as he gained the deck. 'Three points off the leeward bow.' 'How far?' 'About a league, sir; heads same as we do. There she blows!' added the man, as he came slowly down the shrouds, with his eyes fixed intently upon the spouting herd. 'Keep her off two points! Steady! steady, as she goes!' 'Steady it is, sir,' answered the helmsman. 'Weather braces a small pull. Loose to'-gallant-s'ls! Bear a hand, my boys! Who knows but we may tickle their ribs at this rising?'

The captain had gone aloft, and was giving these orders from the maintop-gallant cross-trees. 'There she top-tails! there she blows!' added he, as, after taking a long look at the sporting shoal, he glided down the back stay. 'Sperm whale, and a thundering big school of 'em!' was his reply to the rapid and eager inquiries of the men. 'See the lines in the boats,' he continued: 'get in the craft; swing the cranes!'

By this time the fish had gone down, and every eye was strained to catch the first intimation of their reappearance.

'There she *spouts!*' screamed a young greenhorn in the main chains, 'close by; a mighty big whale, sir!' 'We'll know that better at the trying out, my son,' said the third mate, drily. 'Back the main-top-s'l!' was now the command. The ship had little headway at the time, and in a few minutes we were as motionless as if lying at anchor.

'Lower away, all hands!' And in a twinkling, and together, the starboard, larboard, and waist-boats, struck the water. Each officer leaped into his own; the crews arranged themselves at their respective stations; the boat-steerers began to adjust their 'craft;' and we left the ship's side in company; the captain, in laconic phrase, bidding us to 'get up and get fast' as quickly as possible.

Away we dashed in the direction of our prey, who were frolicking, if such a term can be applied to their unwieldy motions, on the surface of the waves. Occasionally a huge shapeless body would flounce out of its proper element, and fall back with a heavy splash; the effort forming about as ludicrous a caricature of agility, as would the attempt of some over-fed alderman to execute the Highland fling.

We were within a hundred rods of the herd, when, as if from a common impulse, or upon some preconcerted signal, they all suddenly disappeared. 'Follow me!' I shouted, waving my hand to the men in the other boats; 'I see their track under water; they swim fast, but we'll be among them when they rise. Lay back,' I continued, addressing myself to my own crew, 'back to the thwarts! Spring *hard!* We'll be in the thick of 'em when they come up; only *pull!*'

And they did pull, manfully. After rowing for about a mile, I ordered them to 'lie.' The oars were peaked, and we rose to look out for the first 'noddle-head' that should break water. It was at this time a dead calm. Not a single cloud was passing over the deep blue of the heavens, to vary their boundless transparency, or shadow for a moment the gleaming ocean which they spanned. Within a short distance lay our noble ship, with her idle canvass hanging in drooping festoons from her yards; while she seemed resting on her inverted image, which, distinct and beautiful as its original, was glassed in the smooth expanse beneath. No sound disturbed the general silence, save our own heavy breathings, the low gurgle of the water against the side of the boat, or the noise of flapping wings, as the albatross wheeled sleepily along through the stagnant atmosphere. We had remained quiet for about five minutes, when some dark object was descried ahead, moving on the surface of the sea. It proved to be a small 'calf,' playing in the sunshine.

'Pull up and strike it,' said I to the third mate; 'it may bring up the old one—perhaps the whole school.'

And so it did with a vengeance! The sucker was

transpierced, after a short pursuit; but hardly had it made its first agonised plunge, when an enormous cow-whale rose close beside her wounded offspring. Her first endeavour was to take it under her fin, in order to bear it away; and nothing could be more striking than the maternal tenderness she manifested in her exertions to accomplish this object. But the poor thing was dying; and while she vainly tried to induce it to accompany her, it rolled over, and floated dead at her side. Perceiving it to be beyond the reach of her caresses, she turned to wreak her vengeance on its slayers, and made directly for the boat, crashing her vast jaws the while in a paroxysm of rage. Ordering his boat-steerer aft, the mate sprang forward, cut the line loose from the calf, and then snatched from the crotch the remaining iron, which he plunged with his gathered strength into the body of the mother as the boat sheered off to avoid her onset. I saw that the work was well done, but had no time to mark the issue, for at that instant a whale 'breached' at the distance of about a mile from us, on the starboard quarter. The glimpse I caught of the animal in his descent, convinced me that I once more beheld my old acquaintance, Mocha Dick. That falling mass was white as a snow-drift!

One might have supposed the recognition mutual, for no sooner was his vast square head lifted from the sea, than he charged down upon us, scattering the water into spray as he advanced, and leaving a wake of foam a rod in width, from the violent lashing of his flukes.

'He's making for the bloody water!' cried the men, as he cleft his way towards the very spot where the calf had been killed. 'Here, harpooner, steer the boat, and let me dart!' I exclaimed, as I leaped into the bows. 'May the "*Goneys*" eat me if he dodges us *this* time, though he were Beelzebub himself! Pull for the red water!'

As I spoke, the fury of the animal seemed suddenly to die away. He paused in his career, and lay passive on the waves, with his arching back thrown up like the ridge of a mountain. 'The old sog's lying to!' I cried, exultingly. 'Spring, boys! spring *now*, and we have him! All my clothes, tobacco, every thing I have got, shall be yours, only lay me 'longside that whale before another boat comes up! My *grimky!* what a hump! Only look at the irons in his back! No, don't *look*— PULL! Now, boys, if you care about seeing your sweethearts and wives in old Nantuck!—if you love Yankeeland—if you love *me*—pull ahead, *won't* ye! Now, then, to the thwarts! Lay back, my boys! I feel ye, my hearties! Give her the touch! Only five seas off! *Not* five seas off! One minute—*half* a minute more! Softly—no noise! Softly with your oars! That will do.'

And as the words were uttered, I raised the harpoon above my head, took a rapid but no less certain aim, and sent it, hissing, deep into his thick white side!

'Stern all! for your lives!' I shouted; for at the instant the steel quivered in his body, the wounded leviathan plunged his head beneath the surface, and, whirling around with great velocity, smote the sea violently, with fin and fluke, in a convulsion of rage and pain.

Our little boat flew dancing back from the seething vortex around him, just in season to escape being overwhelmed or crushed. He now started to run. For a short time, the line rasped, smoking, through the chocks. A few turns round the loggerhead then secured it; and with oars a-peak, and bows tilted to the sea, we went leaping onward in the wake of the tethered monster. Vain were all his struggles to break from our hold. The strands were too strong, the barbed iron too deeply fleshed, to give way; so that whether he essayed to dive or breach, or dash madly forward, the frantic creature still felt that he was held in check. At one moment, in impotent rage, he reared his immense blunt head, covered with barnacles, high above the surge; while his jaws fell together with a crash that almost made me shiver; then the upper outline of his vast form was dimly seen, gliding amidst showers of sparkling spray; while streaks of crimson on the white surf that boiled in his track, told that the shaft had been driven home.

By this time the whole 'school' was about us; and spouts from a hundred spiracles, with a roar that almost deafened us, were raining on every side; while in the midst of a vast surface of chafing sea, might be seen the black shapes of the rampant herd, tossing and plunging, like a legion of maddened demons. The second and third mates were in the very centre of this appalling commotion.

At length Dick began to lessen his impetuous speed. 'Now, my boys,' cried I, 'haul me on; wet the line, you second oarsman, as it comes in. Haul away, shipmates! why don't you haul? Leeward side—*leeward!* I tell you! Don't you know how to approach a whale?'

The boat brought fairly up upon his broadside as I spoke, and I gave him the lance just under the shoulder blade. With the exception of a slight shudder, which once or twice shook his ponderous frame, Dick lay perfectly quiet upon the water. But suddenly, as though goaded into exertion by some fiercer pang, he started from his lethargy. Making a leap towards the boat, he darted perpendicularly downward, hurling the after oarsman, who was helmsman at the time, ten feet over the quarter, as he struck the long steering-oar in his descent. The unfortunate seaman fell, with his head forward, just upon the flukes of the whale, as he vanished, and was drawn down by the suction of the closing waters, as if he had been a feather. After being carried to a great depth, as we inferred from the time he remained below the surface, he came up, panting and exhausted, and was dragged on board, amidst the hearty congratulations of his comrades.

By this time two hundred fathoms of line had been carried spinning through the chocks, with an impetus that gave back in steam the water cast upon it. Still the gigantic creature bored his way downward with undiminished speed. Coil after coil went over, and was swallowed up. There remained but three flakes in the tub!

'Cut!' I shouted; 'cut quick, or he'll take us down!' But as I spoke, the hissing line flew with trebled velocity through the smoking wood, jerking the knife he was in the act of applying to the heated strands, out of the hand of the boat-steerer. The boat rose on end, and her bows were buried in an instant; a hurried ejaculation, at once shriek and prayer, rose to the lips of the bravest, when, unexpected mercy! the whizzing cord lost its tension, and our light bark, half filled with water, fell heavily back on her keel. A tear was in every eye, and I believe every heart bounded with gratitude at this unlooked-for deliverance.

Overpowered by his wounds, and exhausted by his exertions and the enormous pressure of the water above him, the immense creature was compelled to turn once more upward for a fresh supply of air. And upward he came, indeed; shooting twenty feet of his gigantic length above the waves by the impulse of his ascent. He was not disposed to be idle. Hardly had we succeeded in baling out our swamping boat, when he again darted away, as it seemed to me, with renewed energy. For a quarter of a mile we parted the opposing waters as though they had offered no more resistance than air. Our game then abruptly brought to, and lay as if paralysed, his massy frame quivering and twitching as if under the influence of galvanism. I gave the word to haul on; and seizing a boat-spade, as we came near him, drove it twice into his 'small,' no doubt partially disabling him by the vigour and certainty of the blows. Wheeling furiously around, he answered this salutation by making a desperate dash at the boat's quarter. We were so near him, that to escape the shock of his onset by any practicable manœuvre, was impossible. But at the critical moment when we expected to be crushed by the collision, his powers seemed to give way. The fatal lance had reached the seat of life. His strength failed him in mid career, and sinking quietly beneath our keel, grazing it as he wallowed along, he rose again a few rods from us, in the side opposite that where he went down,

'Lay around, my boys, and let us set on him!' I cried, for I saw his spirit was broken at last. But the lance and spade were needless now. The work was done. The dying animal was struggling in a whirlpool of bloody foam, and the ocean far around was tinted with crimson. 'Stern all!' I shouted, as he commenced running impetuously in a circle, beating the water alternately with his head and flukes, and smiting his teeth ferociously into their sockets, with a crashing sound, in the strong spasms of dissolution. 'Stern all! or we shall be stove!'

As I gave the command, a stream of black clotted gore rose in a thick spout above the expiring animal, and fell in a shower around, bedewing, or rather drenching us, with a spray of blood.

'*There's the flag!*' I exclaimed; 'there! thick as tar! Stern! every soul of ye! He's going in his flurry!' And the monster, under the convulsive influence of his final paroxysm, flung his huge tail into the air, and then, for the space of a minute, thrashed the waters on either side of him with quick and powerful blows; the sound of the concussions resembling that of the rapid discharge of artillery. He then turned slowly and heavily on his side, and lay a dead mass upon the sea, through which he had so long ranged a conqueror.

'He's fin up at last!' I screamed, at the very top of my voice. 'Hurrah! hurrah! hurrah!' And snatching off my cap, I sent it spinning aloft, jumping at the same time from thwart to thwart, like a madman.

We now drew alongside our floating spoil; and I seriously question if the brave commodore who first and so nobly broke the charm of British invincibility, by the capture of the Guerriere, felt a warmer rush of delight, as he beheld our national flag waving over the British ensign, in assurance of his victory, than I did, as I leaped upon the quarterdeck of Dick's back, planted my wafe-pole in the midst, and saw the little canvass flag, that tells so important and satisfactory a tale to the whaleman, fluttering above my hard-earned prize.

The captain and second mate, each of whom had

been fortunate enough to kill his fish, soon after pulled up, and congratulated me on my capture. To get the harness on Dick was the work of an instant; and as the ship, taking every advantage of a light breeze which had sprung up within the last hour, had stood after us, and was now but a few rods distant, we were soon under her stern. The other fish, both of which were heavy fellows, lay floating near; and the tackle being affixed to one of them without delay, all hands were soon busily engaged in cutting in. Mocha Dick was the longest whale I ever looked upon. He measured more than seventy feet from his noddle to the tips of his flukes, and yielded 100 barrels of clear oil, with a proportionate quantity of 'head-matter.' It may emphatically be said, that 'the scars of his old wounds were near his new,' for not less than twenty harpoons did we draw from his back—the rusted mementos of many a desperate rencounter."

THE OCEAN.

Roll on, thou deep and dark blue Ocean—roll!
Ten thousand fleets sweep over thee in vain;
Man marks the earth with ruin—his control
Stops with the shore;—upon the watery plain
The wrecks are all thy deed, nor doth remain
A shadow of man's ravage, save his own—
When, for a moment, like a drop of rain,
He sinks into thy depths with bubbling groan,
Without a grave, unknell'd, uncoffin'd, and unknown.

His steps are not upon thy paths—thy fields
Are not a spoil for him—thou dost arise
And shake him from thee; the vile strength he wields
For earth's destruction, thou dost all despise,
Spurning him from thy bosom to the skies,
And send'st him, shivering in thy playful spray
And howling to his gods, where haply lies
His petty hope in some near port or bay,
And dashest him again to earth:—there let him lay.

The armaments which thunderstrike the walls
Of rock-built cities, bidding nations quake,
And monarchs tremble in their capitals—
The oak leviathans, whose huge ribs make
Their clay creator the vain title take
Of lord of thee, and arbiter of war—
These are thy toys, and, as the snowy flake,
They melt into thy yeast of waves, which mar
Alike the Armada's pride, or spoils of Trafalgar.

* Thy shores are empires, changed in all save thee—
Assyria, Greece, Rome, Carthage, what are they?
Thy waters wasted them while they were free,
And many a tyrant since ; their shores obey
The stranger, slave, or savage; their decay
Hath dried up realms to deserts:—not so thou!
Unchangeable, save to thy wild waves' play!
Time writes no wrinkles on thine azure brow—
Such as creation's dawn beheld, thou rollest now.

Thou glorious mirror, where the Almighty's form
Glasses itself in tempests; in all time,
Calm or convulsed—in breeze, or gale, or storm—
Icing the pole, or in the torrid clime
Dark-heaving;—boundless, endless, and sublime—
The image of Eternity—the throne
Of the Invisible; even from out thy slime
The monsters of the deep are made; each zone
Obeys thee; thou goest forth, dread, fathomless, alone!

BYRON.

THE END.

www.ingramcontent.com/pod-product-compliance
Lightning Source LLC
Chambersburg PA
CBHW032136160426
43197CB00008B/671